CliffsNotes™

Investing in the Stock Market for Canadians

by Marguerite Pigeon and C. Edward Gilpatric

IN THIS BOOK

- Learn what it takes to be a successful investor
- Get up to speed on stock market terminology
- Research and select promising stocks
- Choose the right broker or online trading service
- Build and adjust your portfolio as the stock market changes
- Reinforce what you learn with CliffsNotes Review
- Find more stock market information in CliffsNotes Resource Centre and online at www.cliffsnotes.com

CDG Books Canada, Inc.

CDG BOOKS
CANADA

About the Authors

Marguerite Pigeon is an author and journalist whose titles include *Shopping Online For Canadians For Dummies* and the forthcoming *Investing For The First Time for Canadians*. She's worked as a writer, photographer, reporter, and producer for several news organizations including CTV and CBC Radio and CBC Television.

C. Edward Gilpatric earned a Ph.D. from the University of Chicago. He is a former registered stock representative and spent many years as an audit manager and director for the state of Illinois.

Publisher's Acknowledgements

Editorial

Senior Project Editor: Mary Goodwin
Acquisitions Editors: Joan Whitman, Mark Butler
Copy Editor: Liba Berry
Technical Editor: Joanne Follows

Production

Project Coordinator: Donna Brown
Text Production: Kyle Gell Art & Design
Proofreader: Martha Wilson
Indexer: Wendy Thomas

CliffsNotes Investing in the Stock Market for Canadians
Published by
CDG Books Canada, Inc.
99 Yorkville Avenue
Suite 400
Toronto, ON M5R 3K5
www.cdgbooks.com (CDG Books Canada Web site)
www.cliffsnotes.com (CliffsNotes Web site)
www.idgbooks.com (IDG Books Worldwide Web site)

Canadian Cataloguing in Publication Data
Pigeon, Marguerite
  Investing in the stock market for Canadians

(CliffsNotes)
Includes index.
ISBN 1-894413-12-1

1. Stocks — Canada. 2. Investment's — Canada. I. Gilpatric, C. Edward (Clarence Edward), 1930–. II. Title. III. Series.
HG5152.P53 2000   332.63'22'0971   C99-932653-8

Printed in Canada.

1 2 3 4 5 TRI 04 03 02 01 00

Distributed in Canada by CDG Books Canada, Inc.
For general information on CDG Books, including all IDG Books Worldwide publications, please call our distribution centre: HarperCollins Canada at **1-800-387-0117**. For reseller information, including discounts and premium sales, please call our Sales department at **1-877-963-8830**.
This book is available at special discounts for bulk purchases by your group or organization for resale, premiums, fundraising and seminars. For details, please contact our Special Sales department at **1-877-963-8830** or Email: spmarkets@cdgbooks.com.
For authorization to photocopy items for corporate, personal, or educational use, please contact Cancopy, the Canadian Copyright Licensing Agency, One Yonge Street, Suite 1900, Toronto, ON M5E 1E5; Tel: **416-868-1620**; Fax: **416-868-1621**; www.cancopy.com

Table of Contents

INTRODUCTION

The stock market is probably not a completely foreign concept to you, but you may not know enough to buy and sell stocks with confidence — or have a commitment to long-term investing. You need this book because

■ You're interested in the stock market, and you want to learn the essentials quickly.

■ You want to invest for your lifetime goals, but you worry about the risk.

■ You've heard that you can potentially make more money in the stock market than the interest you receive on your savings and chequing accounts.

Your first trip to the bookstore or public library can be an overwhelming and dismaying experience. So many choices, so little guidance. The value of this book is that it has everything to get you started investing in the stock market — except the specific stocks that *you* are going to select.

Why Do You Need This Book?

Can you answer yes to any of these questions?

■ Do you need to learn about investing your money in the stock market fast?

■ Don't have time to read 500 pages on the stock market?

■ Do you need to get more return on your money than the 1% (or even less) that a typical savings account offers?

■ Do you need help figuring out what all those confusing terms like *IPO, total market value,* and *preferred stock* mean?

If so, then CliffsNotes *Investing in the Stock Market for Canadians* is for you!

How to Use This Book

You're the boss here. You get to decide how to use this book. You can either read the text from cover to cover or just look for the information you want and put the book back on the shelf for later. Here are a few ways that we recommend you search for a topic of interest:

- Use the index in the back of the book to find what you're looking for.

- Flip through the book looking for your topic in the running heads at the top of the page.

- Look for your topic in the Table of Contents in the front of the book.

- Look at the In This Chapter list at the beginning of each chapter.

- Look for additional information in the Resource Centre or test your knowledge in the Review section.

- Or, flip through the book until you find what you're looking for — since we organized the book in a logical, task-oriented way.

Also, to help you find key information quickly in the book, you can look for icons strategically placed in the text. Here is a description of the icons you'll find in this book:

If you see a Remember icon, make a mental note of this text — it's worth keeping in mind.

If you see a Tip icon, you'll know that you've run across a helpful hint, uncovered a secret, or received good advice.

The Warning icon alerts you to something that could be dangerous, requires special caution, or should be avoided.

Don't Miss Our Web Site

Keep up with the fast-paced world of investing by visiting the CliffsNotes Web site at www.cliffsnotes.com. Here's what you find:

■ Interactive tools that are fun and informative.

■ Links to interesting Web sites.

■ Additional resources to help you continue your learning.

At www.cliffsnotes.com, you can even register for a new feature called *CliffsNotes Daily,* which offers you newsletters on a variety of topics, delivered right to your e-mail inbox each business day.

If you haven't yet discovered the Internet and are wondering how to get online, pick up *Getting On the Internet,* new from CliffsNotes. You'll learn just what you need to make your online connection quickly and easily. See you at www.cliffsnotes.com!

CHAPTER 1

DETERMINING YOUR FINANCIAL NEEDS AND GOALS

IN THIS CHAPTER

- Deciding whether to pay outstanding debts or invest your money
- Setting your investment goals
- Committing to a savings and investment plan

Anyone who can earn the money to start an investment program can successfully invest in stocks. In this chapter, we walk you through some personal issues you need to resolve before you begin investing. Should you invest your money or pay off your debts? What are your specific financial goals? Can you commit to an investment plan? Get ready to do some serious thinking — and acting — but don't worry, this chapter can help put you on the path to achieving your personal financial goals.

Doing a Reality Check: Are You Free of Major Debt?

Before you consider any type of investment plan, make an honest appraisal of your overall financial situation. You may want to pay off some outstanding debts before you begin a savings and investment program.

Because this is a book on investing, we suggest that you look at debt as "reverse investing." When you owe money, whether to a person or an institution, the lender is making money off of you. If you're constantly paying more in interest to some lender than you're making on your savings and investments, you're going backward in your hopes of building your nest egg for a secure and comfortable future.

Not all debt or borrowing is bad, however. You may have borrowed money for your education. You probably got a lower interest rate because of government involvement. You expect that your enhanced earning power will more than compensate for the interest you pay on your loan. In many cases, this assumption is true.

The bottom line regarding debt is that it is a drag and a burden until it is paid off. Unless you can convincingly show that borrowing money now will increase your ability to earn money in the near future, get rid of your debt as soon as you can so that you can start building up your net worth for the future you dream of.

Don't make the mistake of borrowing money to buy stocks. Don't buy the sales pitch that a particular investment is the opportunity of a lifetime. If you borrow to invest, you incur real debt with no guarantee of possible future gains.

Sizing up credit card debt

Carrying credit card debt is one of contemporary life's easier entrapments. Credit card companies make getting credit and running up big balances simple and alluring. By adding extra fees, some credit cards penalize users who do not carry balances on their card. Credit card companies want you to carry balances — the bigger the better from their point of view. And why not? Credit account interest really pays off for companies issuing cards.

Credit card debt can carry interest charges in the 18 to 22% range. Clear up credit card debt before you even think of investing. No reliable way exists for you to earn more on stock investments, even in the short run, than the rate of interest you're paying on your credit card debt.

Paying off your credit card balances — even a little at a time — is a form of savings. Look at it this way: By paying off only $1,000 a year from a debt of $10,000, you save about $220 at typical credit card interest rates, and your net worth, even though still in negative territory, rises proportionately.

Considering other kinds of debt

If you're fresh out of university or even a few years into your first job after graduation, you may be carrying a heavy load of student loans that require repayment. Check your interest rates. If you're paying in the single digits (below 10%), don't consider these loans as urgent to pay off as credit card debt. Some investments can produce earnings higher than 10%. Therefore, using your money to purchase these investments is wiser than paying off your student loans; you can make more from the investment than you will pay in interest on the loans.

You may also be better off by putting your money into investments rather than paying off your instalment loan debt (for example, your car loan) — *if* you can earn more on the investment than you would pay in interest on the loan.

This holds true for your mortgage as well. If you are using all of your spare money to pay down a mortgage quickly, you may be robbing yourself of the earning potential of those dollars: You are essentially tying up all your money indefinitely.

A better plan would be to negotiate relatively low monthly mortgage payments, and put the balance of the money into an investment, like a stock mutual fund, where your money will earn you money over time. If that investment is inside a registered retirement savings plan (RRSP) you'll reap the added benefit of tax-free growth until you retire. You'll only pay income tax when the money comes out of the registered plan.

While interest on your mortgage is not tax-deductible, you can view interest on home equity loans (really lines of credit) differently. This kind of interest is considered an *investment loan,* meaning Revenue Canada takes account of the fact that the loan money will be used towards investments. Credit card and instalment loan interest are not tax-deductible. Interest on RRSP loans was tax-deductible until 1981, but is no longer so.

Some financial advisers warn against the temptation to use your home equity line of credit to finance your investments, since you do run the risk of losing on those investments — and possibly your home. However, if your investments are relatively safe, it may be a low-cost way to earn money for your retirement. Ultimately, the decision, like many others in the investment world, comes down to your willingness to withstand risk.

Setting Your Goals

Setting goals sounds easy. "I want to be rich and retire by the time I'm 50." But is this statement a goal or a fantasy? More than likely, most statements of this sort are fantasies or dreams. Dreaming is fine, but looking forward to a bright future is not goal-setting. As you begin to formulate your goals, ask yourself three basic questions:

1. Can I break down my general goals into specific objectives?

2. What must I do to realize these specific objectives?

3. Is this a short-term or a long-term goal?

We provide a place in Figure 1-1 for you to list your goals. Consider the following examples. Suppose that your goal is to

- **Retire with financial security.** What does security mean to you? Does it mean that you stay in the home that you have lived in for 30 years? Or does it mean that you can sell that big, old house and move to a luxury condo in Banff? Do you want to retire at 60, 65, or 75? How much money will you need to save every year in order to retire at the time and to the place you prefer? What are your savings options? For example, have you maximized your RRSP contributions?

- **Start your own business.** Do you want to start an independent business or buy a franchise? Can you work out of your home, or do you need to purchase or build a site? How will you pay your bills until the business shows a profit? Can you get a small-business loan? How much money will you need in order to purchase and establish the business (acquire the site, buy inventory, hire personnel, purchase insurance, and so on)?

Figure 1-1: A place for you to list your short and long-term goals.

Short-term goals	$$$	Time frame
☐ _____	_____	_____
☐ _____	_____	_____
☐ _____	_____	_____
☐ _____	_____	_____

Long-term goals	$$$	Time frame
☐ _____	_____	_____
☐ _____	_____	_____
☐ _____	_____	_____
☐ _____	_____	_____

- **Put your child through college or university.** Do you want to send your child on to complete a post-secondary education? Will you be able to take advantage of student loan or grant programs? How old is your child? How much money will you need to save each year until your child graduates from high school?

- **Buy a home.** When do you want to move into a new home? How much do you want to borrow? How much money do you want to put down on your home? Do you want to put at least 25% down to avoid paying for a mortgage insurance policy?

Deciding how much money and time you need

When you set specific investment goals, consider two essential factors:

- The amount of money you plan to accumulate

- The time frame for saving that amount of money (keep in mind whether your goal is a short- or long-term one)

Specifying a time frame is an important part of goal-setting. How do you come up with a time frame that makes sense for the amount of money you plan to accumulate?

For example, if you're saving for retirement, your specific goal may be to maintain a standard of living comparable to what you achieved during your working years. Although you need a comprehensive retirement planning program to take into account all the factors unique to your situation, a basic truth remains: You hope to have annual purchasing power equivalent to your current annual income.

You can forecast a time frame by considering when you hope to retire and by reviewing the significant transitions in your life and family history. Look at yourself and what you want out of life. Do you want to retire at 50? What kind of longevity runs in your family? Does your employment or profession define who you are, that is, would you feel empty or lose self-esteem if you gave up your career? After you arrive at a projected retirement year, determine whether you can save enough money to retire at that age and maintain your current standard of living. Consider the following factors:

- Your projected annual income between now and your preferred retirement age

- The annual rate of inflation

- Anticipated income you will be able to draw during retirement: Canada Pension Plan (CPP), work pension, RRSP funds, and other personal savings

If you can afford to retire at your projected year, your time frame is valid. (If you need help with the numbers, contact a professional retirement adviser.)

To make your investment plan work for you, you not only need to design well-founded, long-term goals, you also have to project realistic time frames for your plan. If your goals are vague, or if your targets in time are ever-moving, you will never muster the discipline to achieve the financial security you seek.

Developing an investment plan to meet your goals and time frames

After you calculate a realistic monetary goal and a reasonable time frame to achieve it, work backward to determine how much money you need to invest on a regular basis to accomplish your goal.

You're bound to quickly realize that the sooner you get started on a systematic savings and investment plan, the more likely you are to realize your dream.

You need to save money in order to have funds to invest. To give you some incentive, Table 1-1 is an illustration of a hypothetical investment plan that shows the impact of compounding the interest on your savings and investments. *Compounding interest* means that you leave all the interest you have earned on your savings or investments in your account and add it to your principal.

Suppose that you save $100 a month for a year. After you have accumulated $1200, you invest that amount in the stock market. Every month you save another $100. Each year on January 1, you add another $1,200, and you do this for 25 years. Your total investment over 25 years is 25 × $1,200, or $30,000.

If your investments provide you a steady return of 8%, you will have accumulated $1,296 by the end of the first year, to which you add an additional $1,200 for a total of $2,496.

If this pattern continues year after year, by the end of the 25th year you will have accumulated $99,945.27. If you use 12% for the compounded annual rate of return, your 25 years of investment grows to $180,400.67.

The Rule of 72 is a handy and reliable way of calculating compounded growth. Suppose that your investment yields a solid annual return of 8%. Divide 8 into 72, and you get 9. An investment that yields 8% annually will double in value in 9 years. Doing the math: If your annual return is 12%, your money will double in 6 years.

Don't be misled by the numbers used in Table 1-1. A rock-solid, unvarying annual return of 8% or 12% is very unlikely. Some years you may do better. Some years not as well. However, an *average* annual return ranging from 8 to 12% is quite possible — and many investors have achieved even better returns over long periods.

Table 1-1: $100 Per Month Compounded for 25 Years

End of Year	8% Interest	12% Interest
1	$2,496.00	$2,544.00
2	$3,895.68	$4,049.28
3	$5,407.33	$5,735.19
4	$7,039.92	$7,623.42
5	$8,803.11	$9,738.23
6	$10,707.36	$12,106.81
7	$12,763.95	$14,759.63
8	$14,985.07	$17,730.79
9	$17,383.87	$21,058.48
10	$19,974.58	$24,785.50
11	$22,772.55	$28,959.76
12	$25,794.35	$33,634.93
13	$29,057.90	$38,871.18
14	$32,582.53	$44,735.65
15	$36,389.13	$51,303.93
16	$40,500.26	$58,660.40
17	$44,940.28	$66,989.65
18	$49,735.50	$76,127.61
19	$54,914.34	$86,462.92
20	$60,507.49	$98,038.47
21	$66,548.09	$111,003.08
22	$73,071.94	$125,523.44
23	$80,117.69	$141,786.25
24	$87,727.11	$160,000.60
25	$99,945.27	$180,400.67

Before moving on, take one last look at the 12% column in Table 1-1. Your money will double every 6 years if the rate of return is 12% a year compounded. In the illustration, however, doubling of the investment occurs about every 5 years because you're adding another $1,200 every year. That means that the $180,400.67 total for the end of year 25 can grow to about $360,000 in another 5 years.

Remember

As you play with these figures, you can see why an early start on a systematic and disciplined investment program is so critical. Five years can make a big difference. Another 5 years of growth under the same assumptions can yield another $360,000.

Making a Commitment to Work for Your Goals

The key to success in the stock market centres on your commitment to achieving your goals. Saying that you'll give investing a try won't do the job. You have to begin with a program that takes some money right off the top of your monthly income. Otherwise, you may be tempted to use your investment money for other purposes. Refer to Table 1-1 for a look at what $100 a month can do for you in the long run. If your goal is more ambitious, plan a higher investment amount, but make the sum doable.

Spelled out another way, investment in the stock market is *deferred gratification.* You put off today's pleasures — eating out, extra rounds of golf, the luxury car that has to be financed, the trip to New Zealand, whatever — for the anticipated return of future security. If you're ready to make that commitment, your next move is to settle on a systematic payment schedule for your investment dollars.

Using payroll deduction

The easiest approach to meeting your financial goals is to make your savings and investment program automatic.

Perhaps your company has a program that enables you to use payroll deduction for depositing directly to your savings account. When the time comes for your annual investment, you take your $1,200 or whatever sum you settled on and invest it wisely. If you don't have access to this type of program, your friendly banker can help you set up a savings account with automatic transfers from checking.

Exercising discipline

Much of the discipline you have to apply to reach your financial goals has to do with controlling your spending. You live in a consumer economy. Every day you face pressures and appeals to spend for this or that, and sometimes for worthy causes. You need a budget and a mindset that will keep you from spending the money earmarked for your savings and investment program.

Follow the first rule of every savings program: Pay yourself first. This discipline isn't as much fun as blowing all your cash the second it lands in your pocket. Just imagine, however, the excitement you can enjoy watching your investments grow.

Practising patience

Beyond discipline, you need patience. No law suggests that stocks only go up. As the legendary financier J. P. Morgan allegedly responded when asked to predict stock market performance, "The market will fluctuate."

If you panic and sell the first or second time your carefully researched stocks take a hit in the market, you will never make much money. In fact, you may not make any. You have to have the patience to ride out inevitable market declines.

Don't expect guarantees. Some of your stocks are going to fall. Some will fall sharply. Most will come back. Be patient.

Over the long haul, stocks produce a return greater than almost any other investment.

Are You Ready?

Here is your final checklist of decisions you need to have made in order to get started in investing in the stock market.

1. Have I set my goals and objectives?

2. Have I determined the amount of money I need to realize my goals?

3. When will my goals be realized?

4. Do I have a strategy for implementing my goals?

5. Have I calculated the required rate of return on my savings and investments?

6. Am I willing to bear a risk?

CHAPTER 2

WHAT YOU NEED TO KNOW ABOUT STOCKS

IN THIS CHAPTER

- Differentiating between common and preferred stocks
- Understanding other labels that are given to stocks
- Exploring the major trading markets for stocks and other financial instruments

One of the biggest challenges of investing in the stock market is just understanding what financial writers, brokers, commentators, and other investors are saying, because so many of the terms are unfamiliar.

You will hear a fair amount about brokers in this book. If you choose to use professional help with your investments, your first point of contact very likely will be a *broker*, a licensed intermediary between buyers and the stock market. With few exceptions, all stock purchases must be handled by stockbrokers — even on the Internet. For more info on brokers, check out Chapter 8.

As a beginning investor, you may hear statements like, "Multiples are way too high," or "It's time to get out of cyclicals. We're due for a recession." How do you make sense out of this jargon? By the time you finish this chapter, you will know more than enough to begin sorting intelligently through the many choices that face new investors.

You may be asking, "Why should I bother myself with all this terminology?" The answer is straightforward: You need a basic investing vocabulary so that you understand what you read and so you can eventually make intelligent choices when you're ready to invest in stocks.

The Many Varieties of Stocks

A *stock* is a share in the ownership of a company. Stocks can be divided into a variety of classifications. You should be familiar with two classifications in particular: legal (or formal) classifications, and descriptive (or popular) classifications.

Legal classifications define your rights as a shareholder. *Descriptive classifications* do not have specific legal meaning but are convenient terms that brokers, financial writers, and others use to explain different types of stock.

Legal Classification: Common or Preferred Stocks

In formal or legal terms, the two main classes of stocks are common stocks and preferred stocks.

■ *Common stock* is, well, the more common type. Ownership of common stock usually entitles its holders to a share of the company's dividends and voting rights at company meetings based on the number of shares held. Owners of common shares are also entitled to a proportionate share of the company's assets if the organization is liquidated. However, common stocks offer no guarantee that any dividend will be paid.

■ A stock is designated as *preferred* when it gives its owner preference over the holders of common stock in receiving dividends and also in being paid a share of the company's assets if the company is liquidated. Preferred stocks generally do not confer any voting rights. All companies offer common stock. Relatively few also offer preferred stock.

Most preferred stocks have fixed, or stated, dividend payments, much like a bond. That means they will have a limited life in which a particular amount is paid to the shareholder at a designated time. A few preferred stocks have a varying dividend and are called *adjustable rate preferred.*

Dividends are not guaranteed with preferred stock, but owners of these stocks have voting rights if a company suspends dividends.

A preferred stock is a more conservative, that is, less risky investment than common stock. The downside of preferred stock is that the holders receive only the stated dividend and do not participate in the company's growth in the same way common stock shareholders may. Table 2-1 shows the pros and cons of common and preferred stock.

Table 2-1:   Common and Preferred Stock

Stock Type	Pros	Cons
Common	Owner shares in success if company profits	Owner is at risk if company falters
Preferred	Owners receive preference over common stock owners in receiving didivends	Dividends don't increase if company prospers

The stock reports printed every day in *The Globe and Mail Report on Business* and *National Post Financial Post,* and other publications identify when a stock is preferred. Because the large majority of stocks are common stocks, there are no listing notes when a stock is common.

Descriptive Classification

After you get past the legally correct terminology used to categorize shares of a corporation (common and preferred stock), you come to a great variety of additional ways to label or talk about stocks outside of common and preferred. *Descriptive* is a broad term that encompasses all of the other labels you can put on stocks. In the rest of this section, we tell you about some of the other labels or categories you will run across when researching stocks.

Three basic descriptive categories are widely used to classify stocks:

- **Total market value:** Stocks are categorized by size, based on the total market value of company stock

- **Anticipated performance:** Categorized by perceived investment potential of the stock

- **Industry group:** Categorized by the nature of the company's business

Total market value

A widely used category to classify stocks descriptively is based on the total market value of the shares of the company whose stock is being traded. *Total market value* or *market capitalization* is a number derived by multiplying the current market price of one share of the company's stock times the total number of outstanding stocks. For example:

Current market price × number of outstanding shares = total market value.

$50/per share × 100,000,000 outstanding shares of stock = $5,000,000,000 total market value

Generally speaking, in Canada, stocks of companies whose total market value is in the $250-million range are referred

Figure 2-1: Total market value determines the cap size of a stock.

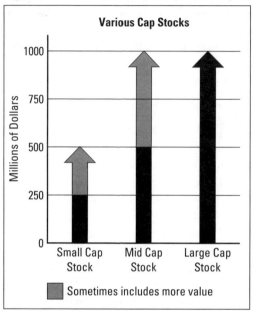

to as *small cap* (see Figure 2-1). Companies whose share value totals between $500 million and $1 billion are called *mid cap*. Those that are $1 billion or more are *large cap*.

Actually, you don't need to calculate the total market value of any company on your own because the work has already been done for you. The best place to get this information is on the Web. Heavy-duty publications like *The Investment Reporter*, *Investor's Digest of Canada* and the U.S.-based *Value Line* also give this information, and so will company quarterly and annual reports.

Almost all the Web sites that provide stock prices will also give constant updates on total market value because this will change every time the market price of the stock changes (see Cliffs-Notes Resource Centre at the back of this book for a list of Web sites). It is not important to know the precise total market value of a company at any given moment, but you should be aware of whether you are looking at the stock of a small company, a large company, or a company that falls in between.

Please note that no universal agreement on the precise boundaries of these cap categories of stocks exists. Moreover, the numbers that define category boundaries are constantly being revised.

Why is it important to know whether the companies whose stock you're considering are considered to be small, mid, or large cap? The labelling of stock by dollar size provides useful clues to risk and to growth possibilities. The smaller the company, the more risky its stock is likely to be. Conversely, large cap stocks tend to be less risky, more likely to pay dividends, and to grow steadily but not rapidly.

If you're looking for stocks that are less risky than the small cap but with greater prospects for rapid growth than the mature, large cap companies, you would do well to concentrate your search on mid cap stocks.

Anticipated performance

Another common way of describing stocks is based on the *anticipated performance of the company over time*. Here are a few anticipated performance labels placed on stocks:

- **Growth stocks:** Stocks of relatively new and rapidly expanding companies

- **Income stocks:** Stocks of established companies that have a history of paying good dividends

- **Cyclical stocks:** Stocks that rise and fall with the business cycle

The labels applied to stocks such as "growth" or "income" refer to the *past* performance of a stock. So, when a stock is labelled "growth" or "income," these companies have either been relatively new or rapidly expanding in the *past* or have paid good dividends in the *past*. These labels are an educated guess of what the stock is likely to do based on hindsight, but do not offer any guarantee of future results.

Here are a few examples of how knowing whether a stock is a growth or an income stock can help you make investment decisions.

■ New investors presumably want long-term growth. For example, for a young person with years to build up a nest egg, there is little point in investing in a stagnant company with steady but small dividends. A young investor is usually in a position to take greater risks in a growth stock in order to earn greater overall returns.

■ Retired investors, on the other hand, are more likely to seek current income, so they move toward stocks that produce a higher level of current income while maintaining or modestly increasing their value. After retirement, when income from employment is no longer available, the mature investor can begin to take dividends in cash rather than reinvesting them in additional shares, making income stocks a good choice.

You may wonder who would want to buy cyclical stocks, which rise in good economic times and fall back in times of recession or depression. Knowing that a stock is cyclical provides useful clues about how the stock will likely perform. If you're inclined to try to maximize your return by buying low and selling high, you may have a strong interest in the cyclicals. You buy them when you think the economy is about to come out of recession or depression, and you sell them when you think the economy is peaking.

Warning

This book does not recommend an investment program based on constantly trading cyclical stocks. Any strategy that calls for constant trading carries high risks along with possible higher gains. You should know, however, which stocks are more likely to fluctuate with the business cycle so that you don't mistakenly buy them in good economic times and sustain heavy losses in even mild recessions.

Industry group

Industry group is another categorization of stocks. An industry group is a way of lumping like businesses together. For example, all Internet stocks, computer hardware manufacturers, and software producers can be grouped together as technology stocks. These categories are helpful if you're seeking to diversify your stock investments.

Diversification — putting your eggs in more than one basket — is a recommended approach to reducing the risk of relying on the performance of stock in one company or industry (something we'll return to in Chapter 8). For example, having all your investments in one category, like technology stocks, is probably not a good idea because if the entire market takes a downturn, then all your investments will be affected negatively.

The industry groups designated by the Toronto Stock Exchange for its TSE 300 Composite Index are the following:

■ Metals and Minerals

■ Gold and Precious Metals

■ Oil and Gas

■ Paper and Forest Products

■ Consumer Products

■ Industrial Products

■ Real Estate

■ Transportation and Environmental Services

- Pipelines
- Utilities
- Communications and Media
- Merchandising
- Financial Services
- Conglomerates

Analysts have devoted years of study to determining how different businesses perform. For example, junior mining companies in Canada have historically been very volatile, as anyone who lived through the Bre-X saga can attest to. At the same time, these companies can also yield very high returns. Basic consumer goods such as food, on the other hand, have much lower profitability but tend to be more stable, especially during economic downturns.

Stocks are also commonly analyzed by comparing them in terms of growth, earnings, and volatility with other companies in the same category. A familiarity with these terms can help you translate the financial pages of your favourite newspaper and sort through the data involved in the process of selecting a few stocks for investment.

 To better understand industry group categories, check out Industry Canada's informative Web site, called Strategis, at www.strategis.ic.gc.ca. Here, you'll find company directories, industry discussion papers, as well as consumer information and statistics.

The Stock Market and Exchanges

As an investor, you really don't need to know the internal workings of the Toronto Stock Exchange, Vancouver Stock Exchange, or any other exchange. Licensed stockbrokers can do all the work for you by locating the appropriate exchange for your trade.

All five major Canadian exchanges (Toronto, Vancouver, Montreal, Alberta, and Winnipeg) have their own requirements for listing a stock. The specifics of these different requirements are not important for you to know, but the fact that a stock is listed on a major exchange is a valuable piece of information.

You should also know that different types of companies list on different exchanges. Knowing where a stock is listed, therefore, can be a factor in your choice of stocks. As a rule, larger companies list their stocks with the Toronto and Montreal stock exchanges, while the Alberta Stock Exchange lists many of the country's junior oil and gas companies. Winnipeg and Vancouver are renowned for their *penny stocks*. The companies offering these shares are small, speculative, and volatile in performance — making for a very risky investment.

All listed stocks have been scrutinized and must file a wide range of reports with the appropriate provincial or territorial regulatory authority, like the Ontario Securities Commission, the British Columbia Securities Commission, or the Quebec Securities Commission. These bodies do not assure you that the stock of any listed companies will serve your investment needs, but they do provide some assurance that the company is reputable.

All of the provincial and territorial securities commissions belong to an association called the Canadian Securities Administrators (CSA). You can access company reports online by visiting a Web site co-sponsored by the CSA at www.sedar.com. The Web site is known by the acronym SEDAR, which stands for System for Electronic Document Analysis and Retrieval (see Figure 2-2).

Figure 2-2: The SEDAR Web site for company reports.

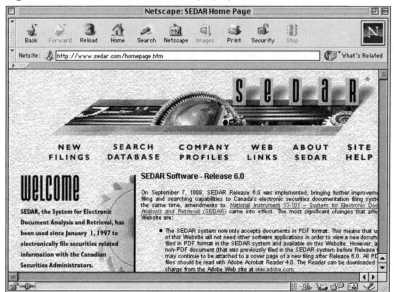

You need to be very cautious if you choose to purchase stocks beyond those listed on the Toronto, Vancouver, Montreal, Alberta, or Winnipeg stock exchanges in Canada, or on the New York Stock Exchange or Nasdaq in the U.S. You almost certainly will be getting into lightly traded stocks — called a "thin market". Brokers take little interest in these shares and do not actively try to sell in these markets.

Understanding IPOs

Another term you may see or hear is IPO. When companies are added to the listings of the major exchanges, they will begin to issue stock for trading on the exchange on which they are listed. This first offer of shares for trading is called an *Initial Public Offering* or *IPO*. IPOs get a lot of attention, and some even generate trading excitement.

When a company goes public and offers its first shares, various brokerages get an allocation of shares that are offered at a price determined by discussions between the company and the various brokerages.

The brokers then let some of their customers know about this new IPO and what the initial offering price will be. Favoured customers of brokerages may have an opportunity to make some quick money if the market price of IPO shares rises sharply.

As a new investor you won't be getting too many chances to get in on IPOs. In fact, unless you've worked with a full-service broker for a while, you're not going to have a chance to buy the IPO shares at the set offering price.

Remember

The important thing for you is not to get beguiled by all the hoopla about IPOs and wish you could be in on the deal. Most IPOs, after an initial surge, drop quickly in price, below even their initial offering price.

CHAPTER 3

INVESTING IN THE STOCK MARKET: REWARDS AND RISKS

IN THIS CHAPTER

- Looking at the different ways of investing your money
- Discovering the risks and rewards of investing

The fact that you've picked up this book and read this far means that you are more than a little interested in getting some real returns on the money you've saved. Before you jump into the stock market with both feet, read this chapter to get a sense of the risks and rewards involved.

Different Ways of Investing in the Stock Market

You have many ways of investing in the stock market. This book deals with only one of those ways, namely, buying stocks on your own for your own personal portfolio.

Investing in stocks for yourself is perhaps the most challenging form of stock investing, but it can also be the most satisfying and possibly the most rewarding.

You have to decide for yourself whether investing on your own is the way to go for you. To help you decide, we list some of the other ways to invest in stocks. You may be surprised — we hope, pleasantly — to learn that you may already be an active participant in the stock market.

Investing as part of a group

There are three principal ways in which you may already be invested in the stock market:

- **As an owner of life insurance.** If you own life insurance, your insurance company very likely has invested some of its reserve funds into various safe investments, including high-quality stocks.

- **As a participant in a company pension plan.** If you're part of a pension plan at work, that pension system will take your dollars along with the dollars of thousands of other employees and invest them in stocks, bonds, and the like.

- **As an owner of mutual fund shares.** A *mutual fund* usually consists of a collection of stocks and bonds, but the fund may also contain other types of securities, such as mortgages, cash accounts, and so forth. (We go into more detail about the pluses and minuses of mutual funds later in this chapter.)

Take a minute to think about money you may have invested in these ways. If you don't already know the details about these investments, ask the people who administer these funds for you to supply you with some background information on them. Doing so is a wonderful way to get a first peek at the stock market.

Investing in stocks on your own

There are two basic ways to buy stocks on your own.

- **Buy stocks in one or several companies and assemble your own personal portfolio.** Almost all the remainder of this book is devoted to this way of investing in stocks.

- **Purchase a package of stocks that someone else has assembled and manages for you.** This package of stocks is a mutual fund.

We give you a quick overview of mutual funds here, but if you are interested in this form of investing, pick up CliffsNotes *Investing in Mutual Funds For Canadians*. A mutual fund is not restricted to owning only stocks, but likely will also have some bonds and cash reserves among its assets. An important aspect of all mutual funds is that they are professionally managed.

Mutual funds offer you a portfolio of carefully selected stocks, a diversified investment option (see Chapter 8 for why this is important), professional management, and the opportunity to invest with minimal cash.

Mutual funds can play an important part of a balanced investment plan, but you need to do careful research to find a fund that will provide a return equal to the stock market as a whole.

The Rewards of Investing

There are many good reasons to invest in the stock market on your own. Among the more common reasons:

- You gain the potential for substantially greater growth and income in stocks than in many other types of savings and investments.

- Your money is available to you as you need it.

- You have greater control of your assets than in a mutual fund.

Greater growth potential

Keeping your money in a regular savings account does provide some return on your money, but you certainly don't get much.

When you receive your next bank statement, be sure to check the interest rates that your bank is paying on your money.

Rates of interest under 1% are the norm these days for daily interest savings accounts. These pitifully low rates of return offer almost no incentive to systematically accumulate assets. Investing your savings or a portion of your savings in stocks can offer the potential for greater growth than placing your money in an average savings account.

If the rate of return you receive on your savings account is close to or below the current inflation rate, you can actually be losing value on savings accounts.

Better accessibility to your money

The money that you invest in stocks that you purchase on your own is available to you whenever you want or need that money. You can simply sell your stock when you're ready to make a major purchase, such as making the down payment on your first home.

While you can cash in stocks or other securities in which you've invested whenever you want, doing so isn't always your best choice. Unless you're facing an emergency, early sale of any investment — including stocks — works against your long-term savings goals. This is especially true if your stocks are held inside an RRSP, where your capital gains and dividends are tax-free until you retire.

Greater control

You also gain greater control over your investments by purchasing stocks on your own. For example, you may be willing to take greater risks to earn greater rewards than many mutual fund managers.

Even at the same level of risk, you have at least a good possibility that you can do better than many fund managers with the research techniques that we introduce in Chapters 4 and 5. Regardless of your performance compared to professional fund managers, you will be free of the 2 to 5% management and other fees that mutual funds commonly charge, and which diminish your overall returns.

The Risks of Investing

Anyone who has even a passing interest in getting into stock investments has very likely heard the conventional wisdom that with patience everybody can make big money in stocks.

Since 1926, stocks listed in the TSE 300 Composite Index have averaged an annual return of just over 10% (*Source: Towers Perrin*). There have been some good years, some bad years, and some great years. When averaged out, whatever money you put in the stock market should double in about seven years or less, or so it would seem.

Despite the impressive historical record of steadily upward-trending performance in the stock market as a whole, you have good reasons to be at least a little bit cautious. Even though the stock market has broken into record territory, there's no certainty about how high — or how low — it may go in the future. Figure 3-1 shows some of the fluctuations in the value of the TSE since 1990.

You could lose a substantial part of your investment

The big and overriding risk in investing is loss of some or — in extreme cases — all the money you've invested. In the worst-case scenario, you can lose everything you invest and incur additional losses in the process!

Tip

If the thought of losing any of your money at all is more than you can bear, please do not consider investing in the stock market. If you're inclined to worry a lot about your money and its safety, invest only in financial instruments of

Figure 3-1: The TSE performance in the 1990s.

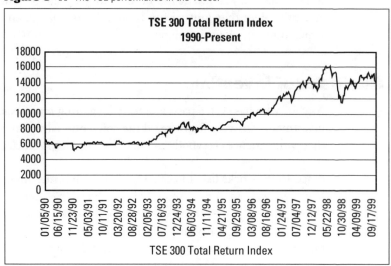

Source: CIBC World Markets

minimal or no risk, such as Guaranteed Investment Certificates (GICs).

You can't see into the future

What makes stock investing both maddening and fascinating is that in the long run, with patience and discipline, you can make some real money, perhaps as much as a consistent 10 to 12% return on your investments. But what nobody knows is when the inevitable downturns will come and how long they will last.

Most of the 1990s have been very profitable for investors. Along the way some stocks have had explosive gains, especially high-tech stocks. Other solid, well-managed, and profitable corporations have shown relatively little gain. Some have even lost ground.

Some losses are short-lived and are quickly recouped, but other sharp drops in the overall stock market can last for years. The most famous was the market crash in October 1929. The market took more than three years to recover losses from that crash.

There is no money–back guarantee

Risk is inherent in stock investing. No federal agency or wealthy corporation insures the money you invest in stocks. You make your choices, and you live with the outcomes.

You don't have total control

Today's economy is a global economy. Events happening on the other side of the planet — events that are totally beyond your control — can influence the stock market. For example, the Gulf War in 1992 led to fears about crude oil supplies, and the stock markets reflected those anxieties.

If the governor of the Bank of Canada decides that inflation is beginning to rise and that the economy is overheating, investors begin to worry about rising interest rates. Sometimes, these concerns cause a decline in stock values.

Information moves quickly these days because of the remarkable advances in communications technology. Even hints that a company's profits may not be up to Bay Street's expectations can lead to sharp losses in the value of individual stocks.

Even the biggest brokerage firms on Bay Street and the large mutual funds managers with all their research and analytic capabilities cannot successfully anticipate every large movement in the market as a whole, much less the swings in value of individual stocks.

The first and last rule for the new investor: Learn how to live with the risks of investing. If you want bigger gains, you must accept more risk. The good news is that there are ways to control and manage your risk (see Chapter 8).

CHAPTER 4

FINDING THE TOOLS TO RESEARCH STOCKS

IN THIS CHAPTER

- Narrowing the range of stocks to research
- Understanding the limits of research
- Finding your comfort level with research
- Locating reliable sources of information on stocks
- Developing a sense for investing in stocks

Enough of the preliminaries, you know the risks of investing, and you're willing to live with them. What comes next?

Now is the time to begin researching your stock investment options. You have over thousands of stocks to sort through and narrow your choice to maybe 25 to 50 to take a closer look at.

Before you begin to feel overwhelmed, there are two things to keep in the forefront of your mind. First, there is no magic or correct number of stocks to research. You may find two or three very promising stocks in your first hour on the Web or in the library. Second, researching stocks is not like solving a math problem. You should be looking for a few good or very good stocks to invest in, not the perfect stock.

Narrowing Your Choice of Stocks

With so many stocks to invest in, you need to narrow your focus down to a manageable number of stocks to research.

Why do you need to do this research? You will want to make sure you have all the information at hand to make the most informative decisions on where to invest your hard-earned money.

Early in your investment career you learn that researching and finding a few good stocks to invest in is a process that never stops. For now, you should narrow your search to 100 stocks if you're working on the Web or 50 if you're working with print media sources. If 50 seems like too many, settle for 25 stocks.

Begin narrowing the field by deciding that you're only going to buy stocks in companies that you understand. This is a key rule to follow. In order to invest in pharmaceutical companies, you don't have to be a biochemist, but you do need to have enough knowledge about what the company does — what its main products or services are — to have a real sense of whether it is likely to be profitable in the long run.

Narrowing the field

With so many stocks to sort through, narrowing the list to only 100 (or whatever other number you want to work with) means that you select only 1% or fewer of all stocks as worthy investment candidates. To get anywhere in this process, you need to settle two issues:

- What will your investment strategy be?

- What screening techniques will you use?

Determining your investment strategy

Review what you learned in Chapter 3 on rewards and risk. Review the investment goals you compiled in Chapter 1. Now ask yourself, "What will it take to get me to my goals?"

Don't just plan your investment strategy in your head. Put your answers on paper. That will bring a much better focus to the task of settling on a strategy so that you can start making choices.

We can't walk you through every investment strategy out there because the options are endless. However, having a sense of what you want financially and how much risk you are willing to take considerably narrows down your choices.

■ **More conservative strategies** focus on mature, very large companies, like those that make up the TSE 100 Index (100 of the largest companies most actively trading on the Toronto Stock Exchange). Nothing is wrong with this strategy, and it has worked well for many people. To find out which companies are listed on the TSE 100, go to the exchange's Web site at www.tse.com.

■ **A less conservative but not totally adventuresome approach** may be to check stocks of large cap companies but exclude very large stocks (for example, those over $2 billion in market capitalization). You can use an Internet stock screener to select stocks only in the $1 billion range using techniques that we describe in detail later in this chapter.

■ **More adventuresome strategies** include mid cap or even small cap companies (refer to Chapter 2 for definitions) whose growth is likely to be more rapid. Again, nothing wrong with these strategies as long as you understand the risks.

If you're working on the Web, using a stock screener can help you locate companies within a specified range of market capitalization. You simply enter a value or range, and the Web site comes up with a list of potential stocks. We explain using stock screeners later in this chapter.

Stock selection is what systems analysts call an *iterative process*: one that is repeated many times, and by force of being such, one that becomes easier over time. In other words, the more times you pick stocks, the more you'll get the hang of it.

Devising a screening technique

You have two ways to screen stocks. You can do it manually or you can do it on the Web. Doing your first screening manually, despite the time it takes, can have some positives. You get a real sense of the range and diversity of stock offerings. Your search may raise some questions such as, why are so many investors paying huge sums for companies with no earnings?

Immersing yourself in detail helps bring clarity to your thinking. You may, for instance, quickly decide that you only want to look at companies that report earnings, or better, a rising trend in earnings. Reading the stock market news in daily national newspapers like *The Globe and Mail* and *National Post*, a weekly like *The Investment Reporter,* or a biweekly like *Investor's Digest of Canada*, makes it very easy to identify which companies are earning money, and whose earnings are rising (or likely to rise).

To make the process of manually sorting stocks to find the 50 or so best for you, buy a copy of *Investor's Digest of Canada* and *The Investment Reporter* — available on some newsstands or at your library. Make sure you have a highlighter to mark those stocks that you want to take to the next level of analysis (see Chapter 5).

Screening stocks by using one of the many programs available on the Web takes a lot less time and, for many, is the preferred way to go.

Several Web programs can do the screening job for you. If you want to look for yourself, begin by visiting Yahoo!

Canada Finance at `http://ca.finance.yahoo.com` for plenty of links and information for the beginning investor.

Or to cut to the chase, visit a site like GlobeInvestor.com at `www.globeinvestor.com` and try out one of the filters (another name for a screener). This service lets you screen stocks based on a percentage change in price over a given period of time. Here's how:

1. Go to the GlobeInvestor.com Web site at `www.globeinvestor.com`.

2. Choose a filter from the left-hand side of the home page. For this example, click the "Historical Prices" filter. (Use the Company Financials Filter to filter companies based on market capitalization.)

3. Choose an industry group from the drop-down list provided, or select "All" to search all industries.

4. Choose a type of security — beginners can stick with common or preferred — from the second drop-down list.

5. Select a specific exchange from the third drop-down list provided.

6. Supply criteria in the appropriate areas provided and click the Go button to begin the filtering process. If you need any help, click the Filters Help link at the bottom of the page.

7. After the process is complete, a results screen lists companies that fit your search criteria.

At the end of your screening process, try to get your list down to something manageable like 50 stocks as potential candidates for purchase. In Chapter 5, we give you further instructions on how to cut your options down further.

Understanding the Limits of Research

In an information age, you may believe that if you just work hard enough, you can find reliable and accurate answers to all your investing questions.

Unfortunately, nobody knows with certainty how the stock market as a whole, or individual stocks in particular, are likely to fare tomorrow — let alone years down the road. The global economy is volatile, and this constant flux has a direct and unpredictable impact on the stock market's upward and downward momentum.

Anybody can pick winners from a field of past performances. With a computer and a database on stocks, you too can assemble a portfolio that, looking back, would have doubled your money every six months. The trick is to pick the winners, the better performing stocks, *beforehand*.

The bottom line for you is this: No amount of research can eliminate all the uncertainties and risks that go into stock market investing. All that research can accomplish is to shift the odds in your favour.

Finding Your Level of Comfort with Research

Unless you have absolutely nothing to do except dig through data on stocks, a reasonable approach to spending time on research should bear some relationship to the dollar amount that you plan to invest. For example, an investment of $10,000 warrants more research than an outlay of $1,000.

Restrain yourself if you're tempted to get carried away with your fact-finding. With so many competing theories, so many available stocks, so many data bits, so much of everything stock-related, keeping your goal in focus can be a challenge.

You're trying to locate a few — certainly no more than ten — different stocks that are going to provide above-average returns for the long run. Are you likely to miss some stocks that could have done even better? Yes, but you will only know that *after* the fact.

Exploring Sources of Reliable Information

Lots of quality information about an astonishing array of stocks is readily available in print and on the Wcb. In fact, you may feel overwhelmed until you're able to focus your research amidst the sea of resources.

In this section, we present a quick guide to sources and the varying levels of information and analysis available at each of these levels.

Stock information of all kinds is available via two major media vehicles.

■ The oldest, of course, is the print medium, the daily newspaper.

■ Ongoing information also appears on a wide variety of online sources. While many Web sites are free, some sites require subscriptions for access.

Better-quality updates provide more than just opening and closing stock prices. More in-depth updates may cost you, but you can also find out things like the extent of change in the stock price, the volume of shares traded, 52-week highs and lows in stock prices, current dividends, yields, and other bits of information.

Don't get caught up in daily or minute-by-minute stock market reports. Market fundamentals do not change by the minute or hour. Stay in focus. You're invested for the long run.

Printed daily stock updates

The daily newspapers in large cities provide the closing prices of stocks for the previous business day along with several other useful bits of data about each stock. The newspapers in smaller cities often restrict their coverage to a small number of heavily traded stocks and/or those of local interest. To make sure that you get at least a reasonable minimum amount of useful information about stocks, stay with the big city dailies.

National circulation dailies are a step up from your local paper. The most prominent of these are *The Globe and Mail* and *National Post*. Each has thorough and well-respected business sections with daily stock listings. For those interested in the U.S. market, you can also pick up *The Wall Street Journal* (WSJ), *The New York Times,* and *Investor's Business Daily* (IBD).

Check out Figure 4-1 to see what a typical stock market listing looks like.

Figure 4-1: Sample stock listing from the daily stock pages of *Financial Post*.

TORONTO 09.28.99

Figures supplied by Star Data Systems Inc.

52W high	52W low	Stock	Ticker	Div	Yield %	P/E	Vol 00s	High	Low	Close	Net chg
1.00	0.33	ABL Cda	ABL			1.9	80	0.37	0.36	0.36	-0.02
n 5.50	4.80	AD Opt	AOP			30.9	3	4.95	4.95	4.95	-0.10
n 9.00	7.70	ADF+	DRX			14.8	12	8.30	8.05	8.30	+0.25
x 9.25	7.40	AEC Ppln	ALB	p0.76	9.6	13.9	369	7.95	7.75	7.95	+0.05
28.10	13.25	AGFMgmtB+	AGF	0.32	1.5	14.7	95	21.10	20.70	21.10	+0.10
11.36	7.65	AGF Master	AFP	3.79	43.1		18	8.80	8.60	8.80	+0.15
11.75	7.95	AGRA Inc	AGR	0.16	1.6	10.6	70	10.50	10.25	10.25	-0.20
1n25.50	21.00	AIC Div	ADC				4	21.00	21.00	21.00	-1.00
x25.60	23.25	AIC of		1.50	6.2		10	24.30	24.30	24.30	+0.05
1.75	0.20	AIT Advd	AIV				43	0.78	0.75	0.75	-0.05
i 16.50	5.40	ALiTech	ALT			21.6	123	5.50	5.40	5.40	-0.05
3.15	1.75	AMR Tech	AMR				69	2.15	1.85	2.15	-0.05
0.40	0.09	AMT Int	AAI				650	0.12	0.12	0.12	+0.02
2.50	1.42	APEX A	AXD			5.5	216	1.80	1.65	1.70	-0.05
x 9.70	7.65	APF Egyun	AY	p1.60	18.7		40	8.60	8.50	8.55	-0.15
n 1.97	0.10	ARC Egy wt	AET				72	1.86	1.80	1.85	-0.01
x 9.35	6.00	ARC Egy un		p1.25	13.5		648	9.25	9.00	9.25	
11.00	6.00	ARC Strat	AEF				10	9.90	9.90	9.90	
11.05	6.25	AT Pistcs	ATP	0.18	2.6	20.0	30	7.00	7.00	7.00	+0.05
98.00	23.50	AT&T Cda	TEL			35.3	281	91.90	91.25	91.70	-0.70
43.75	30.00	ATCO I+	ACO	0.80	1.9	13.3	65	42.00	41.00	41.35	-0.95
27.90	11.20	ATI Tech	ATY			17.9	4089	15.70	15.30	15.65	-0.05
23.50	9.50	ATS Auto	ATA			19.3	359	12.75	12.50	12.75	+0.10
2.00	0.95	AZCAR	AZZ			8.5	184	1.05	1.81	1.05	
n 6.50	4.80	AastraTch	AAH			13.5	63	5.00	4.95	5.00	-0.15
0.88	0.19	Abacan	ABC				3361	0.23	0.205	0.23	+0.02
16.10	6.80	AberRes	ABZ				0491	9.30	9.00	9.25	+0.18
20.55	11.65	AbtibCons	A	0.40	2.3	20.0	12631	16.40	16.80	17.50	-0.05
7.00	5.25	Acanthus	ACR	p0.48	7.9	9.8	5	6.05	6.05	6.05	
11.90	6.00	Acetex	ATX				240	6.00	6.00	6.00	-0.05
0.55	0.22	Adrian	ADL				444	0.30	0.24	0.25	+0.07
0.59	0.15	Advantex	ADX				1766	0.45	0.36	0.45	+0.07
6.20	4.30	AEternat	AEL				2	5.20	5.20	5.20	-0.05
1 13.70	5.60	AgnicoEag	AGE	u0.02	0.3		8226	13.70	11.40	11.40	-0.45
17.25	11.85	Agriumlnc	AGU	u0.11	1.1	12.9	2528	14.40	14.00	14.15	
1.90	0.50	AgroPac A	ADP				2412	0.75	0.75	0.75	
12.85	2.35	Ainswrth	ANS				71	6.55	6.40	6.45	-0.20
11.20	5.10	AirCda	AC				2320	9.90	9.55	9.70	-0.15
10.50	4.50	AirCdaA+					2365	9.35	9.05	9.15	-0.10
5.50	2.30	Airboss	BOS			13.7	97	4.35	4.10	4.30	
11.45	5.80	Akita A+	AKT	0.28	2.7	16.3	60	10.30	10.25	10.25	
48.90	30.75	AltaEnrg	AEC	0.40	1.0	97.0	3608	41.30	40.10	40.75	-0.75
n26.00	24.55	AltaEn pf		2.12	8.3		69	25.45	25.30	25.45	+0.05
54.90	33.60	Alcan	AL	u0.60	1.9	23.6	4256	45.70	44.00	45.60	+0.45
26.10	25.00	AlcanCpf		f1.56	6.1		1	25.95	25.95	25.95	+0.10
24.90	22.40	AlcanEpf		f1.19	5.1		1	23.20	23.20	23.10	-0.95
1.73	0.22	Alexa	AXA				248	1.39	1.26	1.33	+0.02
i 61.00	33.00	AlgomCent	ALC	1.00	2.9	11.8	8	35.00	33.00	35.00	+1.75
3.48	1.63	Algoma5t	ALG				1265	2.09	2.01	2.07	+0.01
5.45	3.80	AlgomMerc	AM	p0.40	8.0		8	5.00	5.00	5.00	
x11.90	9.70	AlgPwr un	APF	p0.88	8.8	25.9	108	10.20	10.05	10.10	-0.15
n25.75	21.50	Aliant	ALP				494	22.00	21.75	21.90	+0.15
26.25	24.70	Allbanc pf	ABK	v1.38	5.5		65	25.15	25.00	25.05	-0.40
38.40	18.05	Allbanc cap					301	23.50	22.20	22.85	-0.20
6.35	2.00	AllbxBlo	AXB				438	3.65	3.05	3.05	-0.60
29.50	17.25	AllncAtlA	AAC				z50	20.00	20.00	20.00	
i 29.50	14.00	AllncAtlB+					1653	14.60	14.00	14.55	-0.05
20.75	13.00	AllnceFrst	ALP				1966	17.15	16.75	16.75	-0.25
1.49	0.74	AlpineOil	ASL				234	1.38	1.23	1.24	-0.08
0.60	0.83	Altai	ATI				64	0.35	0.35	0.35	+0.01
n 1.40	0.61	AltaQuest	AQF				60	0.85	0.85	0.85	
1.38	0.415	AltaRex	AXO				45469	0.85	0.78	0.85	+0.07
3.00	0.75	AmerAtwl	AMZ				271	2.45	2.39	2.39	-0.01
0.455	0.10	AmerBulln	ABP				385	0.25	0.14	0.20	+0.06
4.50	1.45	AmerECO	ECX				59	1.51	1.45	1.45	-0.20
1.13	0.025	AmerGem	GEM				4070	0.56	0.51	0.51	-0.05

The best way to get a feel for the kind of information available in print is to buy a copy of *The Globe and Mail* or *National Post*. Spend some time familiarizing yourself with stock listings.

Televised daily stock updates

If you want to check the stock market in progress, you can tune into Canadian programs like Newsworld Business News (NBN), CTV NewsNet's twice-hourly business updates, or Report On Business Television (ROB TV). For a global perspective, try American cable programming (channels like CNN and CNBC). What you typically see is the stock market ticker for the TSE, the NYSE and NASDAQ moving across the lower half of the screen.

This ever-moving electronic version of the original stock market ticker tape usually displays at short intervals various stock market averages, showing their daily gains and losses — often in real time, as the stocks are being traded.

The big problem with TV coverage of the stock market is that you can sit in front of the screen for an hour and never see stocks that you're watching or investing in. Generally, TV coverage is good for a quick overview of market conditions. Look for shows that provide commentary on the stock market in general and breaking news that can affect the markets.

Online daily stock updates

Daily stock updates via the Internet are impressive. Many free Web sites display stock averages using a 15-minute delay. If you need even more instantaneous information, you can subscribe to special Web sites. A few of the many free and subscription Web sites are listed in CliffsNotes Resource Centre at the end of this book.

As a beginning investor, however, you rarely need this kind of up-to-the-minute information. When the time comes for you to place an order to buy or sell stock, your broker can give you the current market value of each stock.

Web sites, besides providing an abundance of information on an ongoing basis, also offer an array of long-term data on individual firms. By clicking a few buttons, you can obtain recent news stories about a stock, charts showing fluctuations in the price of shares over varying time periods, some analytic reports, and brokers' recommendations for the stock, among other things.

A good place to start your Web search is to visit a gateway site that provides links to many other sites that provide information on stocks. One of the most popular gateway sites is Yahoo! Canada at www.yahoo.ca.

Weekly and other reports on stocks

As you move from daily to weekly or longer reporting, you can expect to gain better balance and perspective. You also widen your view to more trend analysis.

Among the more reputable and impressive sources of stock information is *Investor's Digest of Canada*, a biweekly tabloid. Magazines such as *Canadian Business* (a bi-weekly publication), *Money Sense* (published eight times a year), and *IE:Money* (bimonthly) focus less on the stock market but still have good, readable sections on investments, market trends, declining and emerging sectors, and so on. *IE:Money* is an especially good magazine to read if you want to keep current on many aspects of personal finance, not merely on the stock market.

Don't subscribe to papers or magazines for the prime purpose of tracking the stock market. The subscription costs of a combination of only one paper and one magazine may exceed $200 a year; $200 could represent the annual return on a small investment portfolio. Go to your public library and save your money to buy stocks.

When you move beyond newsstand offerings or the periodicals available at your discount bookstore, you jump into the pricey subscription services. The established Canadian weekly *The Investment Reporter* and the U.S.-based publication *Value Line* are examples of specialized periodicals that offer an endless array of specialized investor information. Be warned: Annual subscription prices are very high for this kind of publication — $250 and up.

A good question is, where can you find suitable reading material to develop your sense of the market? Our answer is in your public library, university library, or possibly in your corporate library.

The company you work for may subscribe to a wide range of general business magazines. If these are circulated, don't be shy about asking to be added to the list.

Several business-oriented magazines are well worth reading, not for investment guidance but for developing your knowledge and awareness of trends in the world economy. Specifically, we recommend

- *Canadian Business* (big-picture)
- *The Economist* (international focus)
- *IE: Money* (focus on personal finance)
- *Fortune* (U.S. publication)

After you narrow your choice of stocks to 100 or fewer, you may want to consult the particularly serious guides like *The Investment Reporter, Money Digest, Blue Book of Stock Reports, Financial Post Investment Reports,* and the U.S.-based *Value Line* in your public or university library.

CHAPTER 5

SELECTING STOCKS

IN THIS CHAPTER

- Capitalizing on your experience to help you choose investments
- Using your intuition to help pick stocks
- Setting criteria when analyzing a company's stock
- Practising stock tracking and investing

Getting started as a do-it-yourselfer in investing in stocks is a challenge and maybe even a bit scary. This chapter helps you sort through the mountain of information confronting you by helping you set criteria for your stock selection.

So that you don't get lost in the research process, the following outline our recommended process for researching — and ultimately selecting — stocks.

1. Make sure you have a list of 50 to 100 stocks. The techniques we describe in Chapter 4 can help you come up with this list.

   You must settle on an investment strategy and write it down. Your investment strategy helps you concentrate on only certain kinds of stocks, based mainly on size and risk.

2. Do some preliminary screening, either manually or with assistance from a Web stock screener. Your resulting list of stocks may be as few as 25 or as many as 50.

3. Review your list and ask yourself: Which of the selected companies do you understand? About which of these companies can you make a fair and reasonable call about their future profitability? Make some cuts in your list as appropriate.

4. Check out a few mutual funds whose investment goals match yours (aggressive growth, capital appreciation, and so on). Note carefully what stocks the better funds contain. Were any of these stocks on your list? Do some of the same stocks keep coming up that are not on your list? If so, add them to your list for further review.

5. Review your list again. Can you cut out 10 or 15 to get down to a more manageable number to work with? Do it if at all possible.

6. Take your list to the library or to the Web. Research the eight criteria that we describe later in this chapter for each stock on your list. Compare the results of your research. You may be able to drop as many as half the names on your list at this point.

7. One way or another, get your list down to no more than ten stocks as prime candidates for purchase.

8. Check the Web or the library for everything you can find about these stocks. Keep notes on anything that supports the future profitability for the company.

9. Bite the bullet and select one to three stocks. Either play the Paper Game (see later in this chapter) or actually buy them (see Chapter 6 for how to do this).

Your goal is to use the tools and research resources that we identify in this book to cut your list of potential stocks to invest in from 50 or so down to fewer than five candidates for actual purchase, possibly to only one for your first year's investment.

Using Your Experience

Never buy a stock in a company or industry that you don't understand. For example, say that you've heard or read that Internet stocks are going crazy and you want to get in before the big surge ends. Suppose that you don't even have e-mail and don't have a clue what a hyperlink is. Do you really think you're qualified to be investing in Internet stocks?

Before you jump on the bandwagon of Internet stocks (or any "hot stock" for that matter), develop some understanding of what the company's product is, whether the company has any staying power, or whether an industry as a whole is compelling and has growth potential.

A good place to find out about a company's products and services is in its annual report. You can get a copy of any company's annual report in several ways. You can

■ Call or write the company and ask for a copy of the most recent annual report.

■ Go to the company's Web site and request or download the most recent annual report.

■ Visit SEDAR (System for Electronic Document Analysis and Retrieval) at www.sedar.com. At this site, you can view annual and quarterly reports, as well as mandatory filings, like the company's prospectus.

Without a grasp of an industry as a whole, you're investing blindly. Just because a stock with no earnings is being bid up by speculators hoping for quick profits that is not a good reason to buy any stock.

The question that should be foremost in your mind whenever you review material about a company is whether the company will likely be increasingly profitable in the long run. The more you know about a company, its products, and its industry, the better you can attempt to answer this key question.

Using Your Intuition

Having experience or education in a particular technology or hot area of research isn't always necessary to find good investment options. Often, basic familiarity is a good starting point for building knowledge through further research. You're a consumer of different products each and every day. You know whether you like or trust a product. You know which restaurants, department stores, and banks you visit and which ones you avoid. You know the services you rely on, and the ones you don't. Try this exercise:

1. Ask yourself what areas, or *sectors,* of economic activity you have some feel for as a consumer. Start with some obvious ones: food, clothing, transportation, housing, travel, health, entertainment, communications, and so on.

   For example, with regard to clothing, you read that XYZ Mart is now a stock market favourite and its stock is set to take off. You've shopped at XYZ Mart but did not enjoy the experience or the quality of goods at the store. As you consider buying the stock, take into account your experience with XYZ Mart as well as other retail department stores.

2. Make a list of companies whose products you believe are high-quality and fairly priced — the very things you look for in every purchase.

   For example, you probably own a car — or at least ride in one. You can select a few car manufacturers and add them to your potential investment list for further analysis.

3. Don't forget to look at service industries, too.

For example, you probably deal several times a week with a bank or two. What have your experiences been with various banks? Which ones do you hear or read good things about? Ask yourself the same questions about airlines, entertainment options, and insurance companies you've recently encountered.

The bottom line: Don't be afraid to rely on your own intuitions and experiences to help you determine which stocks to research and possibly purchase.

Reaching beyond Intuition: What Are the Experts Doing?

You can quickly and easily find out what the investment experts are doing by simply watching what mutual fund managers are investing in. For example, you may have heard or read about the huge increase in Internet stock prices. You may have read that some analysts believe that much of this activity is sheer speculation. You can watch mutual funds that invest in Internet stocks and see how they performed.

How do you find out about a mutual fund's performance? You request the fund's prospectus from a broker or mutual fund Web site. A *prospectus* is a detailed overview of the investments in a mutual fund, written according to government guidelines. After you have the prospectus of a fund you're interested in, look at the stocks the fund managers are investing in and how successful they've been (see Figure 5-1). For more detailed information about mutual funds, pick up a copy of CliffsNotes *Investing in Mutual Funds for Canadians.*

Figure 5-1: Sample stocks a mutual fund is investing in.

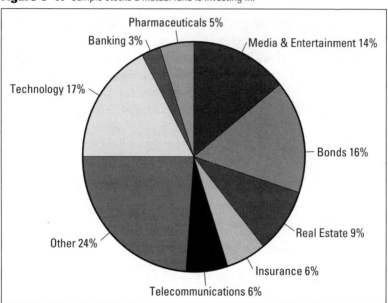

How do you find a list of mutual funds? In the financial pages of *The Globe and Mail* and *National Post,* as well in many other sources like local newspapers and Web sites, you can find lists of mutual funds and their current performance.

Prospectuses are free and available by contacting mutual fund companies by a toll-free call or looking for the mutual fund online. Table 5-1 gives a short list of mutual fund companies and their contact information for you to get started.

Table 5-1: A Starting Point for Mutual Fund Companies

Fund	Phone Number(s)	Web Site Address
The Investment Funds Institute of Canada	416-363-2158; 416-985-7025	www.ific.ca

Table 5-1: A Starting Point for Mutual Fund Companies (continued)

Fund	Phone Number(s)	Web Site Address
AIM Funds Management Inc.	800-588-5684; 416-408-2222	www.aimgt.ca
AGF Funds Inc.	800-268-8583; 416-367-1900	www.agf.com
Altamira Investment Services Inc.	800-263-2824; 416-507-7000	www.altamira.com
Atlas Funds	800-463-2857	www.atlasfunds.ca
BPI Mutual Funds	800-263-2427; 416-861-9811	www.bpifunds.com
Caldwell Investment Management Inc.	800-256-2441; 416-593-1798	www.caldwell mutualfunds.com
C.I. Mutual Funds Inc.	800-268-9374; 416-364-1145	www.cifunds.com
CIBC Securities Inc.	800-465-3863; 416-351-4444	www.cibc.com
CT Investment Management Inc.	800-268-8777; 416-859-5946	www.canadatrust .com
Clarica Life Insurance Co. (formerly The Mutual Group)	800-864-5463	www.clarica.com
Ethical Funds Inc.	877-ETHICAL; 604-714-3800	www.ethicalfunds .com
Fidelity Investments Canada Inc.	800-263-4077; 416-307-5300	www.fidelity.ca
First Canadian Funds Inc.	800-665-7700; 888-636-7687; 416-956-2271	www.bmo.com/ fcfunds
Global Strategy Financial Inc.	800-387-1229; 416-966-8667	www.globalstrategy funds.com
Investors Group Inc.	204-943-0361	www.investorsgroup .com

continued

Table 5-1:   A Starting Point for Mutual Fund Companies (continued)

Fund	Phone Number(s)	Web Site Address
Iris Group of Funds	800-565-6513	www.laurentianbank.com
Mackenzie Financial Corporation	888-653-7070; 416-922-5322	www.mackenzie financial.com
Perigee Investment Counsel Inc.	888-437-3333; 416-860-0616	www.perigeeinvest .com
Royal Mutual Funds Inc.	800-463-3863	www.royalbank.com /rmf/index.html
Sceptre Investment Counsel Ltd.	800-265-1888; 416-360-4826	www.sceptre.ca
Scotia Securities Inc.	800-268-9269; 416-866-2014	www.scotiabank.ca
Spectrum United Mutual Funds Inc.	877-732-8786; 416-352-3000	www.spectrum united.ca
Standard Life Mutual Funds	800-665-6237	www.standardlife.ca
Synergy Asset Management Inc.	888-664-4784; 416-202-6060	www.synergyasset .com
TD Asset Management Inc.	800-268-8166; 416-982-6432	www.tdbank.ca/ mutualfund/ newindex.html
Templeton Management Limited	800-387-0830; 416-957-6000	www.templeton.ca
Titan Investment Management Corp.	800-298-0428; 416-222-1381	www.titan investment.com
Trimark Investment Management Inc.	800-387-9841; 416-228-5500	www.trimark.com
Yield Management Group	888-964-3533	www.ymg.ca

After you read the prospectuses of several mutual funds, narrow down your choices to at least five to ten mutual funds that invest in stocks you're interested in. Study how the stocks have performed and use this as a guide to how the experts invest in the stock market.

In addition to reading mutual fund prospectuses, you can also read up on what the experts are saying. As you browse the papers and periodicals in your local library, be sure to take at least a passing glance at analysts' columns. Often, this kind of commentary mentions individual stocks or classes of stocks that are on the way up or down. Make a list of some of these stocks and do some research.

Picking Stocks: Some Criteria

As a new investor in the stock market, base your investment strategy on long-term increases in stock value. Follow the first rule of stock purchasing: Buy stocks that are good values at the time of purchase and that promise above-average growth for the foreseeable future.

Close observation of a company's *fundamentals* can help you identify stocks of good value. In brief, *fundamentals* are the key indicators of the financial health of the company.

The fundamentals can help provide you with an accurate picture of how much the company is earning, whether these earnings are a solid return on the money investors have put into the company, and whether the company seems able to maintain a steady, upward trend of solid earnings.

Some aspects of a company's fundamentals to pay attention to include:

- The company's quarterly and annual performance
- The company's management team and style
- The company's interest in and financial commitment to researching and developing new products

The Investment Reporter, Investor's Digest of Canada, Money Digest, Blue Book of Stock Reports, and *Financial Post Investment Reports,* as well as the U.S. publication *Value Line,* provide some very useful narrative information about company fundamentals, in addition to offering lots of statistical data.

You can add to our preceding list of fundamentals as appropriate. Each additional bit of data can add some new insight into a stock's underlying value. A word of caution — extended analyses, however, can require you to spend a lot of time gathering data and cause burnout — paralysis by analysis.

Our recommendation is that you focus on eight readily available and easily understood measures or criteria of a company's fundamental value. The goal of going through the same eight criteria for each company is to answer the question: Is this a good company for me to invest in for the long run? As you research, look at the following specific eight criteria:

You may be concerned that researching all the following fundamentals will take hours of your time. Don't worry. In almost all cases, the work has already been done for you. The complete stock reports that you find in *The Globe and Mail Report on Business* and *National Post Financial Post* report some of the following information every day. For more detailed analysis, you will have to go to your public or university library and check specialty publications like *The Investment Reporter, Investor's Digest of Canada, The Money Letter, Money Digest, Financial Post Investment Reports,* and *Blue Book of Stock Reports.* And don't forget to check Web sites on the Internet. They contain a gold mine of information! See the Web sites listed in the Resource Centre at the back of this book.

1: EPS: Earnings per share

The first bit of information you need to know about a company is how much money it is making. For ease of comparison among companies, earnings are universally expressed as *earnings per share* (EPS). These earnings are what's left from gross revenues after expenses, taxes, bad debts, and so on have been subtracted.

For publicly traded and listed companies, these earnings and other financial data come from audited financial records approved by a Chartered Accounting firm.

2: P/E ratio: Price to earnings ratio

The *P/E ratio* shows the relationship between the stock's current price and its reported annual earnings.

A P/E ratio of 20 means that a company earns five cents for every $1 you invest. This does not mean that the company pays a dividend of five cents per share. The company may pay no dividend at all.

The P/E ratio tells us how much you have to pay to buy those earnings per share. In the past, P/E ratios hovered between 10 and 20, but with the surge in stock prices in the 1990s, P/E ratios in the 40 to 60 range and higher are increasingly common.

Generally, the lower the P/E ratio, the more preferable the stock. Profit, another name for earnings, is what drives the price of stocks and payment of dividends.

3: ROE: Return on stockholders' equity

The ROE, or *return on equity,* looks at the company's profitability from a different point of view. This figure tells you what the company has done in the past with the money that stockholders have invested in it.

An ROE of 15% or better is very good and maybe even outstanding, depending on the industry. If you discover in your research that one company's ROE is above 15% and another similar company's ROE is 5%, the company with the higher ROE is clearly the better choice. For a balanced perspective, look at the trends for three or more years.

4: Beta

Beta is a measure of how volatile a stock's price is relative to the stock market as a whole. A beta of 1 means that the stock moves up and down exactly at the same pace as the market as a whole.

A beta greater than 1 indicates that a stock goes up or down faster than the market as a whole. A beta of less than 1 means that the stock's up or down moves are smaller than the market as a whole. Generally, it is a good idea to avoid stocks with betas above 1 because these stocks are more volatile and more risky.

5 and 6: 5-year sales and earnings history

The *5-year sales and earnings histories* each tell you something different. For any stock that you buy, you want to see sales and earnings rise together, with earnings moving upward a bit faster. Earnings that outpace sales usually indicate that the company is becoming more efficient in holding its costs down and in expanding its market.

7: Company size

Why is *company* size important? Generally, if you're looking for maximum appreciation in stock values over time, you want to check out smaller companies where the potential for rapid growth is greater than large established companies (such as those companies included in the TSE 35). Older, larger companies tend to be less nimble and become top-heavy with bureaucracy. The best bets for stronger long-term growth are among the smaller companies, typically those under $250 million in market capitalization.

8: Relative industry strength

You want to look at companies that are ranked at least in the top 25% of their industries — preferably higher.

You can measure *relative industry strength* by comparing stock analyses for similar companies done by periodicals like *Blue Book of Stock Reports, Financial Post Investment Reports,* and the U.S. publication *Value Line.* The analyses in these publications are excellent and are not done by people trying to sell you stocks.

To help you rate the quality of a company's stock, you can copy or modify the chart shown in Figure 5-2.

Figure 5-2: Use this chart to record clues to the quality of a company's stock.

Criteria for Choosing Stocks		
Company Name		
EPS (Earning Per Share)		
P/E Ratio		
ROE (Return on Stockholder's Equity)		
Beta		
5-year sales history		
5-year earnings history		
Company size		
Relative industry strength		

Practising the Business of Real Purchases

Although you're moving closer to your first real investment, you may not realize the work that awaits before your money actually leaves your hands. Here's what you can do to prepare for that day.

Playing the Paper Game

The Paper Game is an exercise that invites you to buy stocks *virtually*, that is, in your head or on a spreadsheet.

1. Start by saving $100 a month. Put it away in some safe place like a bank savings account.

2. When you see or hear of a stock that looks promising, check it out using the eight criteria we just discussed and then *pretend* to buy some shares.

3. Call a discount broker and find out the price of the stock for the day you make your practice purchase. Also, be sure to ask what commission you would be required to pay if the transaction were real.

4. Pretend to buy several other stocks and really put your mind into what you are doing.

Pretend you're actually using your own hard-earned dollars. Note why you're buying each stock and what you expect to gain.

5. Follow your purchases in the daily paper and record their prices once or twice a month. Continue saving $100 each month.

6. As the big day comes for you to make your actual initial stock purchase, review your virtual purchases. How did you do? If the stock rose, was it what you expected? If it fell, can you figure out why?

7. At the end of the year of saving, give yourself a grade. If your portfolio of virtual purchases went up 15%, you're probably ready to buy. If you lost money, rethink your strategy, but don't give up on the stock market.

8. If you have the money to invest, feel you're done playing the Paper Game, and have done research to your satisfaction, narrow your selection down to one to three stocks and buy them — for real.

If the Paper Game is not your thing, still try to identify one to five stocks that look promising. If you're convinced that you've identified one or more quality stocks and feel ready to invest, go for it. But, please, *do not shortcut the necessary research that you should do before you buy anything.*

If you haven't been following stocks until quite recently, make sure that the stock or stocks you buy are more than current "hot" stocks, ones that have experienced a sharp rise in value in the last year. Make sure your first purchase is of stocks that have three to five solid years of performance behind them.

CHAPTER 6

TAKING THE PLUNGE: MAKING THE PURCHASE

IN THIS CHAPTER

- Learning the general procedures for buying and selling stocks

- Trading stocks on the Internet

- Buying stocks without a middleman

- Dealing with the paperwork that goes along with investing in stocks

You have only two ways to purchase stocks: through a stock-broker or by direct purchase from a company. Purchasing stocks through a broker is by far the more common way. Even when you buy stocks online, you still go through a broker or brokerage, even if the whole transaction is conducted electronically.

In this chapter, we walk you through the basic steps involved in starting out and going forward with your stock purchasing plan. We also offer advice on the mundane but critical process of keeping records of your transactions.

Tip

Setting up and maintaining accurate records of every stock transaction is vital. Doing the record-keeping right from the beginning can spare you a lot of headaches in the years ahead.

Buying Stocks with a Broker

The basic process of buying stocks through a broker is fairly simple:

1. **Select a broker and set up an account.** We give you some tips on choosing a broker and setting up an account in the next two sections.

2. **Place an order with the broker.** You place an order simply by calling the brokerage, telling the broker the stock you'd like, and supplying your account number. You also need to explain the circumstances under which you'd like the brokerage to purchase the stock, which we cover in "Understanding different types of orders".

   In some cases, you receive immediate confirmation of your order placement, along with a recital of the charges involved. In other cases, executing your order may take a while, and your broker will call you back to tell you when the purchase was completed and at what price.

3. **Pay for the purchase.** How much you owe right away depends on whether you set up your account as a cash account or a margin account. We explain the difference between the two in "Picking an account type," later in this section.

If you're selling a stock, the process is much the same. Call the brokerage, tell the broker what you'd like to sell, arrange to get the stock certificates to the brokerage (if the brokerage isn't holding them for you), and tell the order taker how you'd like to receive the money — either in a cheque in the mail, as a credit to your account, or as a credit toward another transaction.

Choosing a broker

What should you look for in a broker? Brokers come in two types:

■ **Full-service brokers.** *Full-service brokers* provide advice as part of their fees, and they generally have local offices. Ideally, you work with one associate in the office, someone who tries to get to know you and your financial goals. Some of the more prominent full-service firms in Canada include Merrill Lynch, Nesbitt Burns, Scotia McLeod, RBC Dominion, CIBC Wood Gundy, and TD Evergreen. But this is far from an exhaustive list. Look in your phone directory under "Stocks" for more brokerages.

■ **Discount brokers.** Discount brokers essentially do nothing but take orders, so you won't have a company representative to work with consistently; you get whoever answers your toll-free telephone call. The good news is that discount brokerages have less overhead and pass the savings on to you in the form of lower fees. The bad news is that you should not expect discount brokers to assure you that you're making a good or bad purchase. Some of the more prominent discount firms in Canada are Bank of Montreal's InvestorLine, Canada Trust's CT Securities, CIBC Investor's Edge, Royal Bank Action Direct, Scotia Discount Brokerage, and TD Waterhouse.

All stockbrokers charge a fee, or a *commission,* for their services. These fees vary greatly. As part of your stock-buying research, you need to ask several brokers for information about their fees; also, inquire about what you can expect to pay when you sell the shares at some future date. Brokers are more likely to give you a straight answer about their fees if you present them with a specific request — say, for example, the charge for purchasing 100 shares of XYZ Corporation.

Fees are higher on *odd lots* (any order of 99 shares or fewer) than they are for *round lots* (a purchase of 100 shares). Because you may not be able to afford a round lot, you can consider the odd lot option even if it carries a higher fee.

After you survey brokers about their fees, select one broker to process your purchase. You must first set up an account with your broker, even if you're using an online broker. Setting up an account is a somewhat complicated process, but you have to go through it to become a stock investor.

Setting up an account

For sound business reasons and because of federal requirements, stockbrokers typically maintain complete records on transactions and individual investors. Brokers expect you to supply them with certain information when or before you make your first stock purchase.

Although practices may vary somewhat from broker to broker, you can count on being asked to supply most of the following information:

■ Your legal name and your signature and sometimes proof of your signature

■ Your Social Insurance Number and birth date

■ Your residential address and phone number

■ Your employer's name and a stated figure representing your monthly or annual salary

■ Your banking information. Brokerage requirements vary, but this information usually does not have to be very specific.

Full-service brokers will also ask about your marital status and number of dependents, as well as for an estimate of your net worth and a synopsis of your investment goals. Discount brokers are not likely to require the latter two items.

Questions about your income, employment, and so on, may seem unusually intrusive, but brokers have sound reasons to ask. Full-service brokers are required by regulations to provide stock information and recommendations that are appropriate to the customer's situation. This is known as the "Know Your Client" rule.

If you choose not to provide this information or provide piecemeal and partial information, your broker may have difficulty providing you with the quality of service that you expect. In fact, the broker will choose not to work with you.

Types of accounts

One of the questions you can expect to be asked when setting up an account regards what type of account you want. Accounts fall into two basic types:

- **Cash accounts.** *Cash accounts* require that you settle up, or pay for your purchases, within three business days. What happens if your cheque does not get to the stockbroker in three days? Very likely, you get a telephone call from your broker. Brokers do not treat these matters lightly, and if you continue to pay slowly, you're likely to receive some ominous and unfriendly messages about the sale of your stock and your responsibility to make up any deficit. Interest is also charged on any overdue amounts.

  Brokers have minimal latitude with regard to payment. The regulations that brokerages operate under require that they collect from their clients within three business days of purchase. Failure to observe these regulations can result in fines or other penalties for the brokerages.

- **Margin accounts.** A *margin account* allows you to temporarily borrow money from the broker to purchase securities. To do this, however, you must pledge other securities that you already own to cover payments. If you want to set up a margin account, the brokerage digs deeper into your financial status and creditworthiness.

A margin account is not something that a novice investor should get involved with. If the stock's value goes down before you sell, you still owe the broker the balance of the *full* purchase price. When you set up a margin account, the broker supplies — and requires that you sign — a customer agreement that spells out in excruciating legalese what happens if you don't pay up on time or if you fail to pay up.

Whether you're dealing with a full-service or a discount broker, talk to him or her early in your relationship about delivering payments in a timely manner. Many online brokers require that you maintain cash in an account with them prior to placing stock orders. For other brokers, consider sending money in advance to pay for an upcoming stock transaction. Brokerages do pay interest on such funds — at about the same meagre rate that your bank offers.

Deciding what to do with dividends

A *dividend* is simply the per-share amount of the profits that the company distributes to its stockholders. Not all stocks pay dividends, but some stocks pay dividends regularly. What should you do when you get these dividends? You have two basic options. You can change your mind at any time, and your choice does not have to be the same for all stocks. The options are:

- **Take the dividend in cash.** The company can either mail you a cheque or send the money electronically to your bank account.

- **Reinvest the dividend in additional company stock.** Some companies also allow you to reinvest your dividends to automatically purchase more of the same stock. To make all this sound more complex than it really is, the industry has invented a wonderful acronym, DRIP, for *Dividend Reinvesting Program.*

The monthly investment publication *Money Digest* publishes a list of Canadian companies with DRIPs. The very thorough *Blue Book of Stock Reports,* a biweekly publication, also makes note of DRIPs offered by the companies it reports on.

■ **Leave the dividend in your brokerage account for future investments.**

We recommend that you reinvest your dividends. Think back to what we describe about compounding (refer to Chapter 1). If you're working to build a substantial nest egg, either use your dividends to buy additional shares of the same company that paid the dividend or add the dividends to your regular investment savings to purchase other stocks.

Be sure to ask whether you're going to incur any broker's charges with automatic reinvestment of dividends.

All cash dividends that you receive, whether directly from the company or through a broker, are reported to Revenue Canada at the end of the year. The good news is that dividends from Canadian corporations are not treated as ordinary income. That's because dividends are paid out from a company's profits after taxes. The people at Revenue Canada, aware of this situation, avoid double taxation by offering you a *dividend tax credit.* This credit is applied against the earned income you must claim.

To calculate your dividend tax credit, first gross up the amount of your dividends by 25% — meaning you calculate 125% of their value. Next, calculate federal income tax based on the grossed-up amount. Then subtract the dividend tax credit (13.33% of your grossed-up dividends for non-Quebec residents) from that income tax. The resulting amount of income tax will be lower than you would pay on regular income. Because the province of Quebec collects its own income tax, it sets its own rules regarding dividends.

Deciding what to do with certificates

Finally, tell your broker whether you want your stocks registered in your own name or kept in "street name." *Street name* is a term used in the securities industry for stocks that are owned by the investor but registered in the brokerage's name.

If you instruct your broker to hold your securities in street name, you never see the actual stock certificates. If you ask for the stocks to be registered in your name, however, you will eventually receive a stock certificate from the company. There may be a fee for this.

Some customers feel that their stocks are more secure if they can tuck the actual paper away in a safety deposit box. Be assured that your stocks are safe if you choose to keep them in street name, and possibly safer than if you deal with stock certificates yourself. Even if you keep your stocks in street name, most brokerages make sure that you receive annual reports, notices of the company's annual meetings, and miscellaneous other mailings.

Insurance exists to protect Canadian investors against the possibility of brokerages going out of business. It's called the Canadian Investor Protection Fund and we discuss it at length in Chapter 9.

Types of orders

When you call your broker to place an order, you need to be familiar with different kinds of buy and sell orders that you can place. In the following, we describe three basic kinds of orders:

■ **Market orders** tell the broker to buy or sell the stock at the current market price, by far the most common type of order.

- **Limit orders** limit the broker to buying the stock at a specified price or lower, or to selling the stock at a specified price or higher.

- **Stop orders** tell the broker to buy a stock when it reaches a certain price, or to sell when the stock trades at a specified price.

All orders are only good for one day, unless the client specifies a longer time period.

Limit and stop orders are useful in many situations, but especially when you're going to be out of touch with the market or your broker, or when the market is moving swiftly. Specifying an upper limit of the price you are willing to pay for a stock is always a good idea. You don't want to be unpleasantly surprised to discover that the shares you thought you were buying at $20, for example, ran up to $24 before your order was executed.

One downside to setting conditions on your purchase is that they may delay processing of your order. For example, if you're concerned that XYZ stock is rising sharply, you may want to buy only if you can get the stock for under $20 per share. If the stock has risen past that point, the broker holds the purchase until the market falls to $20 a share or below. If the stock remains above your specified purchase price, your broker is likely to call you to ask about your intentions.

Buying Stocks on the Internet

Doing business via the Internet is an ever-increasing activity among investors, and the electronic marketplace deserves equal billing with the old standard way of trading stock.

Table 6-1 contains a sampling of some of the Internet's more prominent Canadian investment sites:

Table 6-1:   Popular Canadian Internet Investment Sites

Company	Web site address
Bank of Montreal InvestorLine	www.investorline.com
CIBC Investor's Edge	www.cibc.com/english/ personal_services/ investing/index.html
Canada Trust EasyWeb	www.ctsecurities.com
Charles Schwab Canada	www.prioritybrokerage .com
E*Trade	www.canada.etrade.com
National Bank Securities InvestTel	www.invesnet.com/ pbnIndex.htm
Royal Bank's Action Direct	www.actiondirect.com
Scotia Discount Brokerage	www.scotiacapital .com/SDB/
TD Waterhouse	www.tdwaterhouse.com

The actual buying of stocks on the Internet is a very simple process. You just follow these few simple steps:

1. Set up an account with an Internet stockbroker. You can make your initial contact either online or over the phone; but either way, you will have to quickly complete the paperwork that we discuss later in this chapter.

    Curiously, Internet brokers operating in cyberspace may be even more inquisitive than full-service, land-based brokers. Because of the impersonal nature of Internet transactions, online brokers have to rely on more specific information to gauge a customer's temperament, character, and financial status.

2. Make arrangements to pay for your purchase(s) beforehand. Some online brokers require that you deposit money in an account with them before you begin buying stocks.

3. Connect with your broker's Web site, and enter your password.

An order screen comes up, and you type in your order. Your broker usually confirms execution of your order via e-mail.

The Internet is far more than just a convenient, hassle-free way of buying stocks. Electronic communication represents a whole new way of approaching investing in stocks. Advantages of dealing on the Internet, compared with the long-standing ways of buying and selling stocks, include:

■ Greater convenience in placing orders, paying for purchases, and tracking your purchases

■ Speedier access to research materials to help guide your stock selection

■ A wider variety of material than you're likely to find in even the best local public libraries

■ Lower commissions on transactions

Warning

Trading on the Internet also has some disadvantages. After you establish an account with an Internet broker, you may discover that the ease of buying and selling stocks causes you to lose focus on your investment goals. You're cruising out there all by yourself, without the benefit of an investment professional who says to you, "Are you really sure that you want to do this?" In addition, you may have trouble sorting out legitimate businesses from the inevitable array of people who use any opportunity to work scams.

Tip

The Ontario Securities Commission (OSC) Web site has a lot of useful buyer-beware information for people trading stocks on the Net. Check out the section called Canadian Securities Administrators (CSA) Information For Investors at www.osc.gov.on.ca/en/Investor/Csa/csa_info.html.

Maintaining Your Records

You're a serious investor who's committed to a long-term financial plan, so you're inclined to keep good records — no matter how high the paperwork piles up. Be assured that maintaining a solid paper trail simply requires that you pay attention and stay organized.

You can expect your broker to maintain adequate records of all your stock purchases and sales, including everything in between, such as stock splits and dividend distributions. Sometime in January of each year, you will also receive a detailed statement of all the information that you need for your annual income tax returns. This is a legal requirement of both your stockbroker and you.

After you open an account, your broker typically provides you with the following materials:

- A copy of the agreement you signed when you set up your account

- A record of each stock transaction as it occurs, showing the number of shares traded, the price per share, and the total price, plus fees and commissions

- Monthly or quarterly reports showing the current value of your stocks, including a record of any dividend distributions

- An annual account statement containing all the information you need for your income tax filings

- Company-generated prospectuses and other materials that profile your particular stock selection

- Brokerage-prepared analytic reports on stocks that interest you or impress your broker

You also receive the annual report of each company whose shares you own either from the broker or from the company directly, plus a notice of shareholders' annual meetings along with a form to vote on various matters. These matters commonly include election of new directors to the board, change of auditors, change of the company's charter, and so on.

Your reaction to this swelling collection of paper may be, "What am I supposed to do with all this stuff?" If you keep everything for your whole investing career, you will need an 18-wheeler to haul it around, so some choices have to be made. Don't consider tossing the heap in the trash. If you do that, you're sure to regret the move.

Keep the first four items on the preceding list, and for every stock you actually purchase, keep company- and broker-generated reports for two or three years. One reason for this is that you can use these reports for comparative purposes. What was projected? How well did the company perform — up to expectations? Or did it perform below expectations?

If you're using a full-service broker, keep the brokerage-generated analyses. These reports commonly contain recommendations such as "Strong Buy," as well as earnings and price projections. You can use this material to track how well your broker is doing his or her job.

Annual reports are often big and glossy, not to mention self-serving. They do, however, contain audited financial reports (see Figure 6-1). This part of the report can help you track the company's performance. Rip this section out and keep it for two or three years. Beyond that time frame, rely on excellent sources like *The Investment Reporter, Money Digest, Blue Book of Stock Reports, Financial Post Investment Reports, Investment Digest of Canada,* and *Value Line* for historical performance data. This kind of reference material is expensive to purchase, so locate a public or university library that has these reports.

Figure 6-1: The IDG Books Worldwide, Inc., annual report.

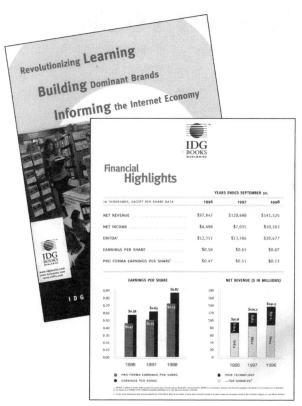

CHAPTER 7
TRACKING YOUR STOCKS

IN THIS CHAPTER

- Setting up a tracking timetable
- Learning what to track in your stock's performance
- Devising a format for tracking
- Continuing your education in stock investing

Tracking is a disciplined program of monitoring a stock to observe its behaviour at different times so that you can make educated adjustments to your portfolio.

Even if the time's not right for you to revamp your stock holdings, tracking or monitoring can produce several useful outcomes, including:

- You can learn a lot about what causes stock movement.
- You can become more educated about the stock market in general.
- You can maintain your motivation to pursue a disciplined and focused investment program.
- You can use your periodic tracking to check on stocks that you considered previously but decided not to purchase. When reviewing these stocks, you may be able to pick up some information about these stocks that you missed earlier.

In this chapter, we explain how you can systematically track your stocks, making the most of your investment time, energy, and dollars, as you gain experience with the flow of the stock market.

Setting Up Your Tracking Timetable

We suggest that you formally track your stock's performance on a quarterly basis. The following list gives you some reasons why regular tracking is important:

- Quarterly tracking is all you need to maintain a well-designed investment program.

- Companies issue their earnings reports on a quarterly basis.

- Companies pay dividends on a quarterly basis.

- Three months is a reasonable interval to collect and file away all the paperwork that comes in for later review.

Corporate earnings reports and dividend announcements do not come out precisely at the end of each calendar quarter. These reports have a tendency to trickle out over several weeks. This unpredictable schedule isn't a concern, unless one or more of the companies in which you're invested begin to have wildly erratic dates for issuing their quarterlies.

You may say, "I enjoy tracking my stocks. It's fun. Besides, I want to be on top of my stocks and the market situation in general." Avoid the temptation to do more than quarterly tracking for the following reasons:

- You may be swayed by daily fluctuations in the value of your stock, leading you to make unwise buying and selling decisions. The underlying fundamentals of the companies worth investing in do not change from minute to minute.

■ You may begin to think that you're going to uncover some key bits of information that others have missed, which is not going to happen. By the time these little gems hit the market, all the big players already know about them. Keep in mind that these folks also act on rumours, wild guesses, speculation, fear, and many other less-than-reliable clues.

Where do you find the information? Go back to the sources that we recommend in Chapter 5 for obtaining basic pre-purchase information. Look to either *The Globe and Mail Report on Business* or *National Post Financial Post*. Information on annual sales and annual earnings, along with calculations of year-to-year changes, appear in more comprehensive publications, such as *The Investment Reporter, Investor's Digest of Canada, Money Digest, The MoneyLetter* or *The Polymetric Report*. Also try the U.S. publication *Value Line*.

Tip

Various Internet sites can help expedite a lot of the work that goes with digging out information on stocks and tracking your portfolio. The list of possible sites is enormous, with new addresses appearing daily. For your initial consideration, check out:

■ i|Money (www.imoney.ca)

■ Quicken.ca (www.quicken.com) — see Figure 7-1

■ GlobeInvestor.com (www.globeinvestor.com)

Some portfolio tracking sites are available by subscription only, but these sites usually come with a free trial. Besides providing assistance with updating the numbers on your stocks, Internet sites also offer links to various company reports and mandatory filings with provincial and territorial securities commissions, analysts' recommendations, current news items, and much more.

Figure 7-1: The Quicken.ca site has news on stocks and can help you track your portfolio.

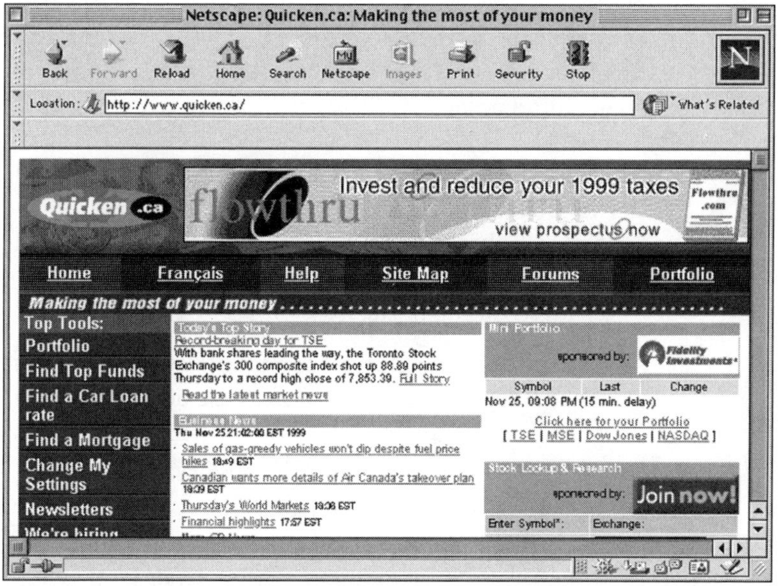

If you have the time, you may consider looking at company press releases on the company's Web site. These reports are also available on some of the many stock quotation Web sites and from Canada NewsWire Ltd., www.newswire.ca and Canadian Corporate News, www.cdn-news.com.

For the truly ambitious, become acquainted with a Web site called SEDAR (System for Electronic Document Analysis and Retrieval) at www.sedar.com. This site contains annual and quarterly reports, as well as many mandatory reports that companies must file with provincial and territorial securities commissions.

Be wary of unattributed, unofficial information on the Internet. Tracking the source of rumours and "facts" on the Internet is next to impossible. Some information is deliberately planted by insiders to stimulate stock movement from which they can profit.

Tracking the Stock

Are you ready to see how your stock is doing? Get out your calculator and scan your financial news sources for the following information:

■ **The stock's price.** Get the opening and closing price for the quarter. Divide the closing price by the opening price, multiply by 100, then subtract 100, and what you've got left is the percentage that the stock's value changed during the quarter.

A positive percentage means that the stock's value increased, while a negative percentage indicates a decrease in value. If you observe too many negative quarters in a row, you may want to consider selling the stock (see Chapter 8).

You also want to find out the high and low price during the quarter. Subtract the low price from the high price to find out the *trading range.* A stock with a narrow trading range is fairly stable, which may or may not meet with your current investment goals. On the other hand, a stock with a wide trading range may be too volatile. If the range is much wider than the market's overall range, you may want to find out what is going on with the company, if you can.

■ **The earnings per share (EPS).** You should be able to find this ratio in any good financial news story about your company's quarterly earnings. If not, the formula is net income minus the preferred stock dividend, all divided by the number of common shares outstanding. You can find these numbers in company reports.

Tracking the EPS over time is a good indicator of the company's progress, but be careful about comparing EPS quarter to quarter because many companies have peak sales seasons that skew the EPS figures. For example, retail stores sell far more during the holiday shopping season than any other time of year. Compare similar quarters to get the most use from the EPS figure.

■ **The price to earnings ratio (P/E ratio).** The basic formula for figuring the P/E ratio is the price of the stock divided by the company's EPS over the past 12 months. Note that because this formula depends on the price of the stock, which changes daily, the P/E ratio also changes daily.

P/E ratios vary from industry to industry, but they can help you size up your company's stock against its competitors. For example, say that Company A and Company B both have earnings per share of $2, but Company A's stock is selling for $18, while Company B's stock is selling for $30. All else being equal, the stock of Company A (with a P/E ratio of 9) is probably a better investment than the stock of Company B (with a P/E of 15), because you're paying less for a stock with the same relative earning potential.

Be a bit wary of reading too much into a P/E ratio. It is an important measure of past performance, but not a reliable indicator of future growth.

■ **Return on equity (ROE).** You can find the ROE ratio in *The Investment Reporter, Money Digest, Blue Book of Stock Reports,* and the U.S. publication *Value Line,* or at some of the Web sites in the Resource Centre at the back of this book. The ROE ratio tells you how well the company is doing with stockholders' invested money. Anything over 15% is very good.

■ **The stock's current beta.** This number is available in the specialized monthly publication called *Money Digest,* available by subscription or at libraries. You may remember from Chapter 5 that beta is an indicator of the stock's risk, and betas do change over time. Make sure that the stock's current beta matches your investment needs.

- **The quarterly dividend figure**. A *dividend* is simply the amount of the company's earnings being paid out to the individual stockholders. Not all stocks pay dividends, even if they have earnings. If a company previously paid dividends, the omission of dividends is a serious sign. For newer, growing companies, failure to pay dividends may mean little or may be positive if earnings are being directed into new product development and expansion of production.

  If dividends were paid, record the "yield" percentage. *The Globe and Mail Report on Business* and *National Post Financial Post* print yield figures daily. So does the *Wall Street Journal* for U.S. stocks.

- **Your total investment**. On each of your updates, add the amount you paid for your stock (your opening investment), the amount of any additional purchases, and the amount of any stock purchased through a dividend reinvestment program (DRIP). The closing total in this quarter becomes your opening investment total in the next quarter.

- **The value of your shares**. The opening value of your stock holdings is the number of shares you had at the beginning of the period multiplied by the previous period's ending share value. The closing value is the current number of shares times the current per-share price. This closing number becomes the opening share value figure for the next quarter.

  To figure your percentage of gain or loss of value for this quarter, subtract the closing value figure from the opening value figure. Divide the gain or loss by the opening value figure, and convert the resulting number — usually a decimal — into a percentage.

Use a calculator to do the math. The numbers aren't always whole numbers in multiples of 10. You may deal with changes such as a total stock value rising from $4,582 to $4,969. The gain in this example is $387. Divide the gain, $387, by the opening period total value, $4,582, multiply by 100, and you get a stock price gain of 8.45%.

We use a chart like the one in Figure 7-2 to keep track of this information about our stocks.

Figure 7-2: A chart for tracking a stock's performance.

	1st Quarter	2nd Quarter	3rd Quarter	4th Quarter	Year-End
Stock Price					
Opening					
Closing					
Percent of Change					
Trading High					
Trading Low					
Trading Range					
EPS					
P/E Ratio					
ROE					
Beta					
Dividends					
Annual Yield					
Investment					
Opening					
Purchases					
DRIP Purchases					
Closing Total					
Value of Shares					
Opening					
Closing					
Percent of Change					

Tracking a Company

Keeping track of the trends in a company's performance is just as important as keeping track of the company's stock. We recommend tracking three important company indicators:

■ Sales

■ The percentage change in sales from last year. (Divide the current sales figure by the previous sales figure, multiply by 100, and then subtract 100.)

■ The company's earnings

Using a chart like the one in Figure 7-3, we keep track of company statistics for a rolling 5-year period. You are, of course, looking for increases every year. If sales or earnings dip, look for an explanation in the company's annual report, or in a specialized publication like *The Investment Reporter, Investor's Digest of Canada, Money Digest, Blue Book of Stock Reports, Financial Post Investment Reports,* or the U.S.-based *Value Line.*

Figure 7-3: A chart for tracking a company's performance.

Sales and Earnings History

Year	Sales	Percent Change from Last Year	Earnings	% Change from Last Year
Current				
Previous				
Two Years Previous				
Three Years Previous				
Four Years Previous				

Companies release sales and earnings figures for two categories: the current quarter ("XYZ Corp. today reported third-quarter earnings of $2.5 million . . . "), and year-to-date or

YTD (" . . . giving the company earnings for the fiscal year of $7.5 million."). Both are usually included in the stories of better financial news sources. We recommend using the year-to-date figures, but the quarterly figures can also indicate trends. Whatever you do, though, make sure that you stick with one or the other. Nothing can foul up a good financial analysis more than mixing apples and oranges.

CHAPTER 8

MAKING MID-COURSE ADJUSTMENTS

IN THIS CHAPTER

- Diversifying your portfolio
- Adding shares through dividend reinvestment programs
- Learning how to adjust your portfolio as the market fluctuates
- Knowing when to sell losers and when to sell winners

Although "buy and hold" is good advice in most circumstances, sometimes you need to make adjustments of one kind or another in your portfolio. You may find yourself too dependent on one type of stock, or you may be trying to figure out how to better budget your stock purchases, or you may want to rethink your dividend selection, or you may even try to figure out whether you should sell a stock.

This chapter addresses some of the issues that arise as you add investments and your portfolio grows.

Diversifying Your Portfolio

If you continue saving a fixed amount each month after your initial stock purchase, in another year's time, you may accumulate enough funds to make another purchase. But before you run out and buy a stock just like the last one you bought, stop and reconsider. The time may be right to diversify.

Diversifying means selecting stocks of different types or sectors. The power of diversification is that you reduce some of the risk of your investments. While one type of stock that you hold goes down, another may be going up, thus reducing the chance of a radical loss of value for your portfolio.

Diversification is not a topic that you need to worry about much when you're starting out. But as you buy more stocks, we recommend that you review your portfolio once a year for balance. Consider these things:

- Do you have too many stocks in one industry? For example, do you have only utility stocks or only Internet stocks? If you're just beginning, this is naturally the case, but as your portfolio grows to, say, nine or ten stocks, try not to have any more than 30% invested in any one industry. If you do, consider selling one of the stocks in that industry, or at the very least, make your next stock purchase from another market segment.

- Look at the betas for the stocks you hold and make sure that you haven't inadvertently loaded up on *high-beta* (very volatile) stocks. You can find out a stock's beta from the monthly publication called *Money Digest* (available by subscription or at libraries) or in the U.S.-based *Value Line*. Make sure that the overall risk rating for your portfolio matches your investment goals.

- Another kind of diversification to consider when your portfolio begins to grow is to put 20 to 30% in bonds. This provides a steady income stream and reduces overall portfolio risk.

- Some analysts believe that you can have a diversified portfolio if you buy a company with a wide range of products and services or if you buy a conglomerate. A one-product company can be hurt badly if the market for its product weakens or if a competitor comes out with a better product.

Continuing to monitor stocks that warranted a first and second look during your original research can help you make good choices when you're ready to diversify.

Purchasing Additional Stocks by Dollar-Cost Averaging

As a new investor, you may want to buy lots of shares in one particular company, but you may not have the money to make a large lump-sum purchase up front. One way to accumulate shares of a stock is to purchase the same dollar amount of the stock each quarter. This is called *dollar-cost averaging*.

Dollar-cost averaging almost always works to your advantage by compensating for the inevitable fluctuations in stock prices. This means that most of the time you end up getting more shares for your money by purchasing stock at constant, equal intervals than if you invest a lump sum equal to all your purchases over several years. Table 8-1 helps illustrate the power of dollar-cost averaging, using four purchases of $300 each during the year.

Table 8-1: A Dollar-Cost Averaging Demonstration

Quarter	Stock Price	What $300 Buys
First quarter	$20	15 shares
Second quarter	$30	10 shares
Third quarter	$10	30 shares
Fourth quarter	$20	15 shares

You end up with 70 shares for $1,200 for an average price of $17.14. If you invested $1,200 initially, you would have purchased 60 shares at $20 each. By spreading out your purchases, you ended up with more shares at a lower price.

Of course, if the price of your favourite stock does nothing but rise all the time, then you're better off buying all the stocks that you will ever purchase right up front. Unfortunately, you have no way of knowing that your stock will only go up, because hardly any stocks do. With dollar-cost averaging, regular, equal dollar purchases of the same stock almost always end up costing you less.

You, the very attentive reader, may recall an illustration earlier in this book that suggested saving $100 a month for a year and then making a $1,200 investment at the end of each year. If buying $300 worth of stock every quarter has benefits over a $1,200, once-a-year purchase, would buying $100 worth every month be even better? Not really. First, just because you can make small purchases is no reason to abandon your overall investment strategy. Keep in mind a couple of things here:

■   You can't buy much stock with just $100 — and stocks are cheaper if purchased in round lots of 100 shares.

■   If you make a lot of small purchases, you may face extra fees that impact your total investment. You may be losing 2 to 3% of your investment to such fees.

■   You will increase your job of record-keeping with lots of small purchases.

If you are accumulating only $100 a month, you probably will be better off investing every three or six months rather than monthly.

Following an overall investment plan that helps you achieve your financial goals is more important than getting $100 or even several hundred dollars invested as soon as you have saved it. Be patient.

Handling Dividends

If you elect to receive your dividend payments in cash (refer to Chapter 6) but are a little disappointed at the slow growth of your portfolio, think again about the company's dividend reinvestment program (DRIP).

Automatic dividend reinvesting has the following advantages:

■ Your investment returns compound.

■ You pick up additional shares without paying broker's commissions.

■ You may even be able to get shares at a small discount.

Many of the companies with DRIPs also allow *optional cash purchases* (OCPs) of additional stock shares beyond those obtained by automatic dividend reinvestment. These OCPs are often available at no commission or with minimal charges that are less than even discount brokers charge.

Despite the advantages of investing through DRIPs and OCPs, you gain no advantage by continuing to buy stock in a company that is going downhill. Make sure that the company's overall performance in terms of sales and profitability remains sound before putting more money into a faltering organization.

Even if the company is doing just fine, DRIPs do carry a couple of negatives:

■ Every time you receive a dividend payment, even if the payment is automatically reinvested in additional shares, you must pay taxes on dividends. That is offset by the fact that Revenue Canada taxes dividends at a lower rate than regular income thanks to the dividend tax credit. For more on the formula for calculating the dividend tax credit, turn to Chapter 6.

■ Keeping records of purchases is a bit more complicated with a DRIP. You're making a series of small purchases, and you must make sure that you record each purchase in appropriate detail: date, amount of purchase, price per share, and number of shares (including the decimals or fractional shares) purchased.

Living with Market Downturns and Stock Losses

Market downturns aren't all that hard to deal with — if you don't panic. Seeing any of your stocks take a big drop is hard on new and seasoned investors alike.

Hard though market downturns can be, control your emotions when they occur. Remember some of the concepts presented in the early chapters of this book:

■ You invested in stocks because you want your money to grow at a faster rate than conservative but lower-yield investments such as Guaranteed Investment Certificates (GICs) and high-quality bonds.

■ The stock market always fluctuates, but over long periods of time the trend has always been upward.

■ Risk is inherent in stock market investing, but you can control levels of risk through proper stock selection and diversification.

Remember

You don't have any gains or losses until you sell some stocks. Until you actually sell a stock, all you have is "paper" gains or losses.

Believe it or not, even the highly paid people who manage billions of dollars panic at bad news, rumours, and natural catastrophes. When the big brokerages and large institutional investors hear news with an uncertain impact, such as an assassination attempt on the prime minister of Canada, their initial reaction is to start selling large blocks of stocks for no apparent or justifiable reason.

So what do you do when the market turns down sharply — for example, more than 2% of its nominal values? Saying what not to do is easy — namely, don't sell automatically.

So far, in its 200-year history, the stock market has always come back. Unless you truly believe that some unimaginable catastrophe is about to befall the world's economies, don't rush to sell your stocks just because the stock market loses 10 to 20% of its value in a few months.

Unless you own nothing but *index funds* (funds that track the stock market as a whole, and rise and fall in step with market rises and falls), don't worry about what the market is doing. Pay attention to what your stocks are doing.

■ If your stock falls when the market falls, that's normal.

■ If your stock falls faster than the market is falling, be alert.

■ If your stock rises when the market falls, count your blessings.

■ If your stock falls when the market is rising, pay close attention. You may have a problem.

Knowing When to Sell a Loser

If your research indicates that you have a losing stock on your hands, you may choose to sell it and cut your losses. Of course, knowing exactly when to sell is easier said than done.

Don't bother to look to books for "the" answer, because one right answer doesn't exist. Just remember to avoid a panic.

Realize that selling a loser (or not selling it) depends at least as much on psychology and intuition as on reason and logic.

In the following list, we suggest how to deal with different scenarios:

■ **A stock's fundamentals are still strong, but recent performance has been poor.** Check the company's fundamentals — namely, its overall performance on such things as sales, earnings, and volatility. (Refer to Chapter 5 for more on company fundamentals.) If the fundamentals are still as sound as when you purchased the stock, don't sell.

Never sell stocks without first checking the company's fundamentals.

■ **The stock's fundamentals have weakened, but not a lot.** Consider selling if your stock is down 10 to 15% from what you originally paid and you feel that the stock is not likely to recover lost ground in the next 12 to 18 months.

■ **The stock is down 25% or more from its original price, and its fundamentals are questionable.** If you don't have a lot of money invested, your risk of further loss is small. Consider riding it out. If you don't have much to lose, you probably don't have much to gain, either.

■ **You plan to take some profits on other stocks.** Consider taking some losses on one or two stocks to offset your gains and save some on your taxes.

Set your own marker — for example, 15% — for the amount of loss that you're willing to live with while you wait for a turnaround. You can also establish a time period for your wait and watch. If your stock doesn't recover some ground in that time period, sell.

Setting up markers for selling on either the upside or downside can take some of the emotion out of a difficult situation. Consider the following scenario: You bought a stock at 50 that has risen to 65, but you see that the company's fundamentals are weakening (as judged by slowing rates of earnings and sales growth). You set your marker to sell at 70 on the upside and 55 on the downside and place limit orders with your broker.

- **A stock had good gains but then had significant losses**. If your stock had a good gain before it started falling, you may want to reset your marker to alert you to a decline off the stock's high, not off its original price.

Knowing When to Sell a Winner

Can you imagine selling a profitable stock? Consider the fact that you have no profits *until* you sell. So when you decide that you have a better use for the money that you have tied up in a stock, even if the stock has been performing well, you sell.

The following are among the good reasons to sell:

- You set a target for growth, and your stock achieved it. You're following a plan.

- Your stock has done well, but growth has slowed to a crawl. The stock isn't what it is used to be. You take your profits and invest in a promising growth stock.

- You need money for the down payment on your retirement dream home or for your kid's university education.

When making a decision to sell or not to sell, don't place much confidence in brokers' and analysts' guesstimations about future or projected earnings and target prices. Experts vary widely on these projections.

Every time you sell a stock, you incur selling costs (broker's charges) and will have to pay tax on your capital gain if you sold at a profit (but at a reduced rate, since Revenue Canada only taxes 75% of capital gains earned annually). If you sold stocks at a loss, the losses can offset some or all of your gains. Check with your tax adviser. You paid taxes all along on your dividends (also at a reduced rate thanks to Revenue Canada's dividend tax credit — more on this in Chapter 6).

CHAPTER 9

WHAT TO DO IF THINGS GO BADLY

IN THIS CHAPTER

- Arming yourself against likely problems and hazards
- Knowing when you have a legitimate complaint
- Understanding your rights as a stockholder
- Seeking recourse when your rights have been violated
- Getting your money back when a brokerage goes belly-up

Everybody's hope when they start buying stocks is that their stocks will go up and never come down. That's not how the world works.

So, what do you do when your plunge into the stock market takes a bad turn? If something goes wrong, the inclination is to seek remedy or redress. These days, lawsuits abound: Everybody seems to be suing somebody. Sometimes, taking legal action makes sense; but filing a suit isn't your only recourse. In this chapter, we offer suggestions for addressing problems that may surface during your lifetime of experiences with stocks and the trading marketplace.

Your First and Best Line of Defence

The first and best rule in the world of stock market business is to check out your broker's recommendations thoroughly. Pay close attention to what you hear and what you read. Don't rely on a single source or single opinion when making important investment decisions.

You're much less likely to get into trouble with any investment decision if you check out the stock's fundamentals before you buy or sell (refer to Chapter 5). This means that you go back and review the vital signs for the last two to eight years.

You certainly will want to look at sales and earnings history, dividends, relative industry strength, and beta or volatility. If you've been doing annual updates on the eight criteria of stock fundamentals (refer to Chapters 5 and 8), you already have this information.

As you read and listen to advice, bear these things in mind:

- Does the person giving you advice stand to profit if you follow the advice? If so, this is a conflict of interest — a big red flag.

- Is a stock touted as a "sure winner" or a "can't miss" opportunity? More red flags. Nobody knows the future. Past performance is no guarantee of future results.

- Does your broker say that you must act today because X or Y or Z is about to happen and a stock is destined to take off? More red flags. Ignore advice like this and get another broker.

- Is a stock recommended on the basis of market timing strategies derived from something called *technical analysis*? Technical analysts study trends, volume, and stock movements, among other things. They then try to predict future market movements on the basis of their analysis of these trends. Extensive studies have demonstrated that technical analysis is worthless in predicting the future.

Because dealings with brokers are likely to be a source of some complaints and misunderstandings, we strongly advise that you and your broker or adviser have a very clear understanding about the extent of services to be provided and the degree of accountability for those services.

Brokers very likely can provide you with a standard printed statement that covers their responsibilities. We're not suggesting that you deal with brokers or advisers as if they were adversaries. Brokers do have a responsibility to provide you with guidance appropriate to your situation, but they do not have the responsibility for the choices you make. See Chapter 6 for tips on selecting a broker.

When Do You Have a Legitimate Complaint?

And the quick answer is, almost never. The following list provides several reasons why legitimate complaints are rarities:

- **The brokers know the rules — and the penalties**. Every reputable brokerage is aware of the risks of exploiting or disserving its clients. All brokers must be licensed and are aware of their obligations to clients. Full-service brokers all know the "know your client" rule, which obligates them to provide stock advice and recommendations appropriate to their client's financial situation and investment goals.

- **Brokerages are very careful about what they promise in their literature**. During the course of researching your investment options, you may receive research reports or other materials from a brokerage. Brokerages spend a lot of money on research, but always issue disclaimers and warnings that past performance does not guarantee future results.

  Phrases like "can't miss" or "opportunity of a lifetime" on these items are grounds for legal action later — but you won't find them on materials from reputable brokerages. You can be certain that the company's legal staff scrutinizes these documents many times before the publications reach you.

In the unlikely event that brokerage documents have misstated a company's financial position or other material matters that would mislead investors, you may have grounds for legal action or other remedy (for example, voiding a purchase of stock).

■ **Your confusion with the highly technical language of a company's financial statements is not a basis for action**. This also applies to the accountant's personal opinion and notes. If you don't understand what you read or if you misread technical language that is beyond your competence, you are on your own.

Don't guess at the meaning of technical and legal documents and use your interpretation as a basis for buying or selling stock. Don't buy stocks that you don't understand and don't take action on any stock you own on the basis of company reports that are over your head.

■ **When you place an unsolicited order with a stockbroker, both full-service and discount, you are on your own**. On unsolicited orders, the broker does not assume responsibility for your actions.

When you become a do-it-yourself investor, you are taking responsibility for your actions.

Two kinds of broker actions are more likely to lead to legitimate complaints and/or successful legal action.

■ **Churning a client's account**. *Churning* is an illegal practice that generates inflated commissions for a broker or other salesperson through excessive trading of a customer's account. The main victims of churning are people who are unable to actively manage their own portfolios and delegate this job to an agent.

■ **Failure of a full-service broker to abide by the "know your client" rule**.

Can you scream and holler at your broker for buying the highly recommended stock that then tanked? Sure you can. Can you expect some form of compensation? Probably not. You may reasonably conclude that you should find a new broker or brokerage, but don't count on much remedy beyond that. Being stung by bad advice should not happen to the diligent investor.

Like any investor, you can have a bad day and not ask the right questions of your broker or not pay attention to what you hear. However, if a broker acts unprofessionally in violation of the rules, the broker can be disciplined. If you believe your broker has been guilty of infraction of his or her responsibilities, you can and should complain. We discuss how to do this later in this chapter.

Investor Rights

As an investor, you have the right to

■ Receive information about your broker and the brokerage firm, including a report on all public record lawsuits, disciplinary actions, and so on. **Note:** This information is available from the Investment Dealers Association of Canada (IDA).

The IDA has four regional offices across Canada. In Toronto, call (416) 364-6133; in Vancouver, (604) 683-6222; in Calgary (403) 262-6393; and in Montreal (514) 878-2854.

■ Receive complete information about the risks and costs of any stock you may buy either from your broker, the company, or both.

■ Receive copies of all agreements between you and your broker, as well as complete and timely account reports.

- Get a clear explanation in non-technical language of the terms and conditions of any stock transaction you enter into with a brokerage.

- Receive complete information about all charges, fees, and commissions connected with your account, including selling charges and account closing charges.

- Recover up to $1 million of lost cash and securities investments if your investment account is held at a brokerage that becomes insolvent. This is the case only if the firm is a member of the Canadian Investor Protection Fund (CIPF). For more on the CIPF, see the section at the end of the chapter called "Insurance Against Insolvency."

Stockholders' rights do not include any guarantee that every stock you buy will live up to your hopes and expectations.

What to Do If You Have a Legitimate Complaint

If you have a legitimate complaint against a brokerage, follow this path to seek a remedy:

1. **Call the broker**. There's no simpler and more effective way to resolve any dispute than starting at the source. A call to your broker may resolve the issue.

2. **Call the broker's boss**. Again, keep seeking a solution at the lowest level possible.

3. **Call the brokerage's compliance department**. A *compliance department* is an internal brokerage department that attempts to resolve disputes brought by investors. Every brokerage is required by law to have at least a compliance function, if not a full-fledged compliance department. You can access the compliance department simply by calling the brokerage or sending a letter. State

your complaint, and you will receive guidance on how to proceed.

4. If the compliance department of your brokerage firm does not satisfy your complaint, you can request arbitration. The arbitration process is set up by the Investment Dealers Association of Canada (IDA) but operates independently. It begins when you send a letter requesting arbitration from the appropriate provincial arbitration firm. (You can get the address from your regional IDA office). Within about 30 days, you and the investment dealer must agree on an arbiter from the roster provided. Within about three months, you will be granted a brief hearing, at which time the matter will be settled. Both sides are allowed to hire legal counsel.

The arbitration panel's decision is *binding,* meaning you waive your right to go to court. The arbiter's decision is final and you must abide by it.

In most cases, arbitration is restricted to disputes about investments worth up to $100,000. Bigger cases will be referred to the courts.

Arbitration is not yet available in the Maritime provinces (although they are working on it). Right now, the process is limited to residents of British Columbia, Alberta, Saskatchewan, Manitoba, Ontario, and Quebec.

If you live in a province where arbitration is unavailable or you don't want to initiate that process, you may, at your own expense, pursue whatever legal remedies you think appropriate. You are certainly entitled to seek redress in any case of fraud or deception. Generally, these cases fall within the jurisdiction of civil litigation. If you have some evidence of criminal action as it relates to your account, complain to the appropriate provincial securities commission.

Remember

No one likes to deal with the dark side of doing business, which can sometimes be unpleasant, even painful. Keeping the following bottom-line thoughts in mind can make your investing experience as pleasant as possible.

- Expect and insist on competence and decent service from those in the securities industry.

- Don't expect to get rich by pursuing action against brokers or companies.

- If you encounter a broker whose conduct is unprofessional, you do yourself and everybody else a favour by bringing the broker's misconduct to the attention of those who can put such a person out of business.

- On the positive side, if you find a broker whose conduct is professional and who you find to be extremely competent in helping you achieve your financial goals, recommend the broker to a friend.

- Last but not least, remind yourself often that managing your money and investing for your and your family's future is serious business that deserves a wholehearted commitment. Give it your best effort, and you very likely will achieve your dreams.

Insurance Against Insolvency

There is no insurance against a bad investment except your own research and prudence. With the stock market, there's always a measure of risk. However, there is a way to get your money back if the brokerage firm you deal with goes under. It's called the Canadian Investor Protection Fund (CIPF), and it covers up to $1 million per customer.

The CIPF is a fund sponsored by the Canadian stock exchanges, the Investment Dealers Association of Canada

(IDA), and its member brokerage firms. Before you sign a new customer agreement with a brokerage, ask about its membership in the CIPF. You can find out more about the fund by visiting its Web site at www.cipf.ca, as shown in Figure 9-1.

Figure 9-1: The Canadian Investor Protection Fund can recoup up to $1 million of your investment dollars if your brokerage becomes insolvent.

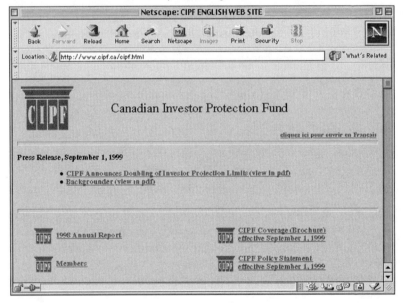

As of September 1, 1999, the CIPF removed the $60,000 limit it used to impose on the cash component of your investment account balance. Now the $1 million coverage simply applies to your total combined cash and securities holdings. If you have an additional RRSP investment account, it is considered separate and is eligible for an additional $1 million coverage.

CLIFFSNOTES REVIEW

Use this CliffsNotes Review to practise what you learn in this book and to build your confidence in doing the job right the first time. After you work through the review questions, the problem-solving exercises, and the fun and useful practice projects, you're well on your way to achieving your goal of investing in the stock market.

Q&A

1. The *stock market* refers to

  a. A building near Bay Street called the Toronto Stock Exchange.

  b. The New York Stock Exchange and Nasdaq.

  c. The sum total of stock trading in Canada and worldwide.

2. Developing a long-term investing strategy

  a. Is not necessary for small investors who own shares in only a few companies.

  b. Gives focus and staying power to your investing plans.

  c. Is a waste of time because the stock market moves in random patterns.

3. Researching stocks before buying

  a. Does not eliminate risk but tilts the odds in your favour.

  b. Is a waste of time because small investors don't have the necessary resources to learn much about any stock.

  c. Is best left to professionals.

4. The commission you pay when you buy stocks

  a. Is the same no matter where or how you buy.

  b. Generally is much lower when you purchase stocks on the Internet than from a full-service broker.

  c. Can be avoided if you purchase from a discount broker.

5. When you buy stocks, you must pay for your purchase

   a. Immediately by prior deposit or electronic fund transfer.

   b. Within ten days of purchase unless you get an extension from the broker.

   c. Within three business days after the stock transaction.

6. Any serious investor will review his/her shares

   a. Periodically through the day through Web sites.

   b. Annually, when preparing tax statements.

   c. At set intervals, but not more often than monthly.

7. If you feel you have been wronged by a broker,

   a. You should contact the compliance department of the broker's firm.

   b. You should assume that you must have made a mistake, so you take your lumps.

   c. You have no resources because there are no guarantees in the stock market.

Answers: (1) c. (2) b. (3) a. (4) b and c. (5) c. (6) c. (7) a.

Scenarios

1. The stock market, as measured by the TSE 300 Composite Index, has fallen almost 5%. You own several stocks, all of which have fallen with the market, some a little faster, some not quite as fast. What should you do?

2. The stock market has risen over 10% this year. You own a stock that pays a decent dividend and has gone up about 6% in the last year. What should you do?

Answers: (1) The best course may be to do nothing. The stock market rises and falls over time and so will your stocks. It is always good to recheck the stock's fundamentals (see Chapters 5 and 8) and find out whether they are holding up to the previous record of earnings. (2) When a stock lags behind the market, you may have reason for concern, especially if the stock's beta (measure of volatility) has been close to 1 in the past. If a stock has made money for you in the past but now seems to be tailing off, selling your stock and putting the money in what might be a better-performing stock may be a good idea. This strategy is an especially good idea if you have some stock losses to offset the gains you made on this stock that is no longer performing up to expectations.

Consider This

■ Did you know that when most people talk about gains and losses in the stock market they really have not experienced either? No one has a gain or loss until they actually sell a stock they own. Until that happens, all they have are "paper" gains and losses. See Chapter 8 for more details.

■ Did you know that if you have a serious complaint against an investment dealer that you can't resolve, you have the option of entering into arbitration? This process (although independent) is sponsored by the Investment Dealers Association of Canada, and it is binding to both parties — meaning you have to live with the outcome. See Chapter 9 for details.

■ Did you know that an investment that yields a constant 8% annual return will double every nine years even if you add no further money, as long as you reinvest all the money your investment earns. If your rate of return rises to 12% a year, your investment doubles every six years. This is called *compounding* or *compound interest*. See Chapter 1 for details.

Practice Projects

1. Go to your library and read a back issue of a periodical that deals with personal finance (for example, *IE:Money, The Investment Reporter,* or *Investor's Digest of Canada*). Get the names of some of the stocks the publication recommended or featured and then check in a paper, such as *The Globe and Mail Report on Business* or *National Post Financial Post,* to find out how those recommended stocks did in a year. Did the results measure up to expectations? If not, can you find clues to why not?

2. While you're accumulating money for your first investment, go to one of the Web sites that tracks portfolios. Create an imaginary portfolio from about five or seven stocks that you have read or heard about as good buys and that you may consider buying yourself. Follow these stocks for three to six months through your portfolio tracker and find out whether you can figure out why they trade the way they do.

CLIFFSNOTES RESOURCE CENTRE

The learning doesn't need to stop here. CliffsNotes Resource Centre shows you the best of the best — links to the best information in print and online about investing. And don't think that this is all we've prepared for you; we've put all kinds of pertinent information at www.cliffsnotes.com. Look for all the terrific resources at your favourite bookstore or local library and on the Internet. When you're online, make your first stop www.cliffsnotes.com where you'll find more incredibly useful information about investing.

Books

This CliffsNotes book is one of many great books about investing published by IDG Books Worldwide, Inc. and CDG Books Canada, Inc. So if you want some great next-step books, check out these other publications:

CliffsNotes Investing in Mutual Funds for Canadians, by John Craig and Juliette Farley. A fast and easy introduction to mutual fund opportunities. CDG Books Canada, Inc., $8.99.

CliffsNotes Investing for the First Time for Canadians, by Marguerite Pigeon and Tracey Longo. Get up to speed on the world of investing. CDG Books Canada, Inc., $8.99.

Investing For Canadians For Dummies, by Eric Tyson and Tony Martin. The perfect book for people looking to develop an investment strategy. CDG Books Canada, Inc., $27.99.

Personal Finance For Dummies for Canadians, 2nd Edition, by Eric Tyson and Tony Martin. A great book to help you manage your financial priorities and plan your investments. CDG Books Canada, Inc., $26.99.

It's easy to find books published and distributed by CDG Books Canada, Inc. including all of the popular lines from IDG Books Worldwide, Inc. You can find them in your favourite bookstores near you and on the Internet. There are four Web sites that you can use to read about our entire line of books:

- www.cdgbooks.com
- www.cliffsnotes.com
- www.dummies.com
- www.idgbooks.com

Internet

Next time you're online (and for those interested in the stock market, that should be relatively soon), try these excellent Canadian Web sites for advice, information, stock quotes, and more:

Bank of Montreal InvestorLine, www.investorline .com. BOM's online discount brokerage.

CIBC Investor's Edge, www.cibc.com/english/personal_services/investing/index.html. CIBC's online discount brokerage.

Canada NewsWire Ltd., www.newswire.ca and **Canadian Corporate News,** www.cdn-news.com are two companies that publish news releases from the corporate world. Both sites catalogue corporate and government press releases.

Canada Stockwatch, www.canada-stockwatch.com. This excellent subscription site has real-time stock quotes, statistics, and news from the Canadian and U.S. stock markets.

Canada Trust EasyWeb, www.ctsecurities.com. Online discount brokerage.

Canoe Money, www.canoe.ca/Money/home.html. Canoe, one of Canada's more popular Web portals, has a very good Money area, where you will find business and stock market news and tools.

E*Trade, www.canada.etrade.com. An online discount brokerage with very low commissions.

GlobeInvestor, www.globeinvestor.com. The freshest news, market updates, charting and stock filtering by industry, price, and historical performance make this site, sponsored by *The Globe and Mail,* ideal for stock market enthusiasts.

i|money, www.imoney.com is a diverse and informative personal finance site with information on just about every money-related topic Canadians could hope for, including up-to-date stock quotes and graphing tools. (This site has a similar name, but is not the same as the magazine *IE:Money,* which also maintains a Web site with a different address, namely www.iemoney.com.)

Investors Association of Canada, www.iac.ca. This non-profit association of individual Canadian investors maintains an excellent Web site, but you'll have to pay to access the full range of services, including back issues of its monthly publication *Money Digest.*

Quicken.ca, www.quicken.ca. This site has excellent learning and investment tools including a portfolio tracker, advice columns from stock market specialists, regular stock quotes, and even access to annual company reports online.

Royal Bank Action Direct, www.actiondirect.com. Online discount brokerage.

Scotia Discount Brokerage, www.scotiacapital.com /SDB/. Online discount brokerage.

SEDAR (System for Electronic Document Analysis and Retrieval), www.sedar.com is the electronic filing site maintained by the Canadian Securities Administrators (CSA) — the association that represents the provincial and territorial securities commissions. Check out SEDAR for company profiles and other mandatory filings by public companies traded on Canadian stock exchanges. You can also access annual and quarterly company reports here.

Sympatico Finance, www.sympatico.ca. Through an alliance with E*Trade Canada, you can use this portal site for its online trading service, or as an excellent starting point for stock quotes and general investment info.

TD Waterhouse Investor Services Canada Inc., www.tdwaterhouse.ca. TD Bank's Internet discount brokerage.

Toronto Stock Exchange, www.tse.com. Canada's biggest stock exchange has a very thorough site, including stock prices, information on its important indices, and even a glossary of stock market–related terms.

U.S. Web sites

There are also some worthwhile U.S. sites you can visit when making stock investment decisions including:

American Stock Exchange, www.amex.com. Office site of AMEX.

DripCentral, www.dripcentral.com. Devoted to explaining the nuances of dividend reinvestment programs, known as DRIPs. Beware that terminology for DRIPs in Canada is somewhat different.

EDGAR (Electronic Data Gathering and Analysis), www.sec.gov/edgarhp.htm. Publishes all mandatory reports that companies must file with the U.S. Securities and Exchange Commission.

New York Stock Exchange, www.nyse.com. Provides stock prices and daily market summaries.

Also next time you're on the Internet, don't forget to drop by www.cliffsnotes.com. We created an online Resource Centre that you can use today, tomorrow, and beyond.

Magazines and Newspapers

To keep current on stock prices, you can consult any large metropolitan daily paper. For more specialized coverage of financial matters, check out the following Canadian publications:

Blue Book of Stock Reports. Each issue of this biweekly specialty publication offers 32 in-depth stock reports, including long-term statistical analysis of each company's operations. An excellent place to explore the breadth of a company's fundamentals.

Canadian Business. For thorough coverage of all aspects of Canadian business, try this namesake biweekly magazine.

Financial Post Investment Reports. These incredibly thorough reports cover the top 500 Canadian public companies, providing historical data and details of the company's current financial picture. If you're thinking of investing in a large-sized Canadian company, you can't go wrong exploring its "FP Investment Report."

Financial Post Magazine. Another upscale monthly, the *FP Magazine* has features on everything from style to serious business coverage.

Globe and Mail Report on Business. Daily stock coverage as well as news stories and features on business in Canada and around the world.

IE:Money. Published six times a year, this personal finance magazine has loads of features on investment, as well as advice on devising good investment strategies. (Not to be confused with the exclusively online personal finance Web site called i|money.)

Investor's Digest of Canada. A bimonthly investment newsletter offering extensive stock analysis and projections.

Money Digest. Published monthly by the Investors Association of Canada (a national non-profit association of individual investors), *Money Digest* has stock recommendations as well as a host of tips on personal finance.

Money Reporter. This weekly newsletter focuses on preferred shares and other income investments.

Money Sense. This is the new kid on the block when it comes to Canadian finance mags. Published eight times a year, *Money Sense* covers a bit of everything from investing to consumer issues, to retirement planning to money itself.

National Post Financial Post. The *FP* was amalgamated into *National Post* when Canada's second national daily was launched in late 1998. Turn here for excellent news and features on the business world, as well as thorough coverage of the market.

Report on Business Magazine. This glossy monthly publication includes long-format business features and various business-related departments. Look for its annual Top 1000 Companies list when deciding where to invest your money.

The Investment Reporter. One of Canada's oldest and most respected investment-related weekly newsletters. Here you'll find stock recommendations and tips on maximizing your portfolio's performance.

The Northern Miner. For anyone even remotely interested in mining, this internationally recognized weekly newspaper covers every aspect of the industry, including news and detailed analysis of mining companies traded on the major Canadian exchanges.

The MoneyLetter. Edited by Gordon Pape, a well-respected investment adviser, this twice-monthly newsletter includes advice for stock market investors and some stock recommendations.

The Polymetric Report. This monthly contains thorough evaluations of a large number of specific common stocks. You'll also get trend analysis for various stock groupings and beta (volatility) ratings.

International magazines and newspapers

An incredibly broad range of finance-related newspapers and magazines also exists outside of Canada. If you're interested in a broad perspective on the U.S. and world markets, check out these well-recognized publications:

Investor's Business Daily. Often referred to as *IBD*, this paper offers the most complete daily updates on U.S. stock market activity. It also incorporates a special rating tool that provides analytic information about individual stocks not available in other sources.

The Wall Street Journal. The *WSJ* is a very good daily paper with international circulation. As its name suggests, it provides detailed coverage of stock market activities along with solid, well-written general news coverage. Sorry, no sports page or comics.

Barron's (weekly). A very readable weekly paper that gives quick and comprehensive coverage to the world of stocks and high finance.

Forbes. Offers solid coverage of business with special sections on stocks and investing.

Fortune. Presents more big, in-depth stories and analyses. Ideal for a general business and economics education. Stocks are not its forte.

Value Line. This pricey publication focuses on very serious investors. Its detailed, authoritative reports on individual companies come out in periodic segments several times a month and will be useful to investors in Canada as well as the U.S.

Send Us Your Favourite Tips

In your quest for learning, have you ever experienced that sublime moment when you figure out a trick that saves time or trouble? Perhaps you realized you were taking 10 steps to accomplish something that could have taken two. Or you found a little-known workaround that gets great results. If you've discovered a useful tip that helped you budget more effectively and you'd like to share it, the CliffsNotes staff would love to hear from you. Go to our Web site at www. cliffsnotes.com and click the Talk to Us button. If we select your tip, we may publish it as part of *CliffsNotes Daily,* our exciting, free e-mail newsletter. To find out more or to subscribe to a newsletter, go to www.cliffsnotes.com on the Web.

INDEX

COMING SOON FROM CLIFFSNOTES

Online Shopping

HTML

Choosing a PC

Beginning Programming

Careers

Windows 98 Home Networking

eBay Online Auctions

PC Upgrade and Repair

Business

Microsoft Word 2000

Microsoft PowerPoint 2000

Finance

Microsoft Outlook 2000

Digital Photography

Palm Computing

Investing

Windows 2000

Online Research

CDG
BOOKS
CANADA

COMING SOON FROM CLIFFSNOTES
Buying and Selling on eBay

Have you ever experienced the thrill of finding an incredible bargain at a specialty store or been amazed at what people are willing to pay for things that you might toss in the garbage? If so, then you'll want to learn about eBay — the hottest auction site on the Internet. And CliffsNotes *Buying and Selling on eBay* is the shortest distance to eBay proficiency. You'll learn how to:

■ Find what you're looking for, from antique toys to classic cars

■ Watch the auctions strategically and place bids at the right time

■ Sell items online at the eBay site

■ Make the items you sell attractive to prospective bidders

■ Protect yourself from fraud

Here's an example of how the step-by-step CliffsNotes learning process simplifies placing a bid at eBay:

1. Scroll to the Web page form that is located at the bottom of the page on which the auction item itself is presented.

2. Enter your registered eBay username and password and enter the amount you want to bid. A Web page appears that lets you review your bid before you actually submit it to eBay. After you're satisfied with your bid, click the Place Bid button.

3. Click the Back button on your browser until you return to the auction listing page. Then choose View⇨Reload (Netscape Navigator) or View⇨Refresh (Microsoft Internet Explorer) to reload the Web page information. Your new high bid appears on the Web page, and your name appears as the high bidder.